THE COOKIE LOVER'S COOKIE BOOK

Also by Richard Sax

Cooking Great Meals Every Day
(with David Ricketts)

Old-Fashioned Desserts

New York's Master Chefs

From the Farmers' Market
(with Sandra Gluck)

THE COOKIE LOVER'S COOKIE BOOK

RICHARD SAX

Illustrations by William Joyce

PERENNIAL LIBRARY

HARPER & ROW, PUBLISHERS, New York
Cambridge, Philadelphia, San Francisco, Washington
London, Mexico City, São Paulo, Singapore, Sydney

The recipe for Maida Heatter's Oatmeal Wafers appeared in *Maida Heatter's Book of Great Desserts,* originally published by Alfred A. Knopf, Inc. © Maida Heatter. Reprinted with permission.

FIRST EDITION

Designer: C. Linda Dingler
Copy editor: Joan Whitman
Indexer: Auralie Logan

Library of Congress Cataloging-in-Publication Data

Sax, Richard.
    The cookie lover's cookie book.

    Includes index.
    1. Cookies. I. Title.
TX772.S29   1986   641.8'654   86-45147
ISBN 0-06-096108-2 (pbk.)

89 90 MVP 10 9 8 7 6 5 4 3 2

This is for my mother

CONTENTS

WHAT'S A COOKIE LOVER?

It's someone who'd rather eat a really good plain butter cookie than the fanciest whipped cream cake.

. . . who can't fall asleep, thinking about those home-baked cookies downstairs just waiting to be enjoyed with a big glass of cold milk.

. . . who'd rather go without lunch, and have a big plateful of cookies and milk instead.

. . . who'd prefer a collection of rich, buttery homemade cookies on his birthday to the best birthday cake in town.

. . . who considers semisweet chocolate chips an important kitchen staple—something to keep on hand all the time.

. . . who welcomes a rainy day as a good chance to stay inside and bake a big batch of cookies.

Probably, it's *you.*

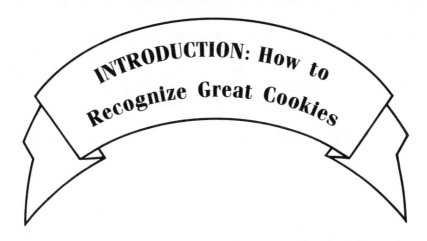

INTRODUCTION: How to Recognize Great Cookies

As a cookie lover, you know that a great cookie has a special flavor. You can't explain what it is, exactly, but you just *know* when it's there. It's the taste of pure vanilla and sweet butter that warms your mouth as you swallow, and the crisp-breaking texture you can get only in a cookie that's baked fresh. When you bite into the perfect cookie, something inside you says, "That's it!"

Cookie lovers have had it good lately—there are outstanding cookies available just about everywhere. And with all the cookies around, it's difficult not to want to give them all a try.

Ever on the lookout for a great cookie experience, you sample the new varieties at the supermarket. Some call themselves "distinctive," and some even maintain that they're just like home-baked (they're not, by a long shot), or promise that they're "so soft, they taste like they're right from the oven." Not bad in a pinch, but they aren't it.

So, dissatisfied, you try the bake-yourself cookies that come frozen or refrigerated—"homemade are just as good," their ads boast. Are they it? Just read through the list of their ingredients sometime. Ingredients should be fresh, wholesome, and in English —butter, eggs, nuts—not artificial, or sound like the contents of a chemistry textbook.

Going on in your quest, you try the chocolate chip cookies at bakeries; some aren't bad—especially when they're made with all butter. But you wouldn't mistake them for your own, right out of the oven.

Then, with hope around every corner, you purchase some at a "cookie shop." People raved about their products when these stores first opened—"wait till you taste them, and wait till you see the *huge* chunks of chocolate!" The cookies at cookie shops can be good, because they're usually made with real butter and good chocolate. (And they should be, when they cost $6 to $8 a pound!) So, although they occasionally taste almost like homemade, they are more often served soft, "just-baked," which usually means underbaked—and who wants to eat a mouthful of raw butter and sugar? Sorry, that *still* isn't it.

So what's the secret of great cookies? *You have to bake them at home.* Sure, it's more trouble, but when you bake cookies yourself, you know that everything that goes into them is of the best quality, and you get an advance treat as the kitchen fills with their unbeatable aroma, and you take care to bake them just right. In fact, baking cookies is as much fun (almost) as eating them.

And when you bite into them, still warm, with a big glass of cold milk, then you finally say,

"That's it!"

WHAT IS A COOKIE?

In Harold McGee's *On Food and Cooking*, a fascinating—and readable—book on "food science," there's an attempt to define what a cookie actually is:

> Given the huge range of products covered by this term, everything from miniature cakes to a hardened sugar syrup to thin, crisp sheets of well-developed glutenous dough, it is impossible to explore cookies in much detail without writing a small book.

Without getting too technical, McGee notes that cookie doughs are proportionally richer in butter (or other shortening) than doughs for muffins, biscuits, or bread. Of the major types of doughs for baked goods, only pastry contains more fat: about 65 percent of the flour by weight for pastry, compared to 40 percent for cookies.

Unlike bread or pastry, though, cookies are rich in sugar (up to 45 percent of the weight of the flour), and are the only type of dough that is also enriched and leavened by eggs, which comprise up to 6 percent of the flour's weight. (Cakes are classified as batters rather than doughs, and are much richer in eggs—up to 100 percent of the flour's weight for spongecake.)

Some cookies are even richer, made with quick puff pastry (see page 96) which contains more butter than flour by weight. Others are made with lean, not-sweet doughs, and are more like crackers (see the chapter called "Not-Too-Sweet Cookies and Crackers" for several examples).

The main thing, for me, that distinguishes cookies from other baked goods is their size. Cookies can be crisp or chewy, plain or wildly rich, iced or not. But they're all baked small, in individual form, and that makes them just right to pop in your mouth.

THE BASIC TYPES OF COOKIES

Cookbooks usually classify cookies according to the way they're made. The basic types are:

1. *Drop Cookies:* The easiest—the dough is dropped onto the baking sheets in spoonfuls. Most popular varieties: chocolate chip, oatmeal, peanut butter.

2. *Bar Cookies:* Baked in a solid sheet in a square or rectangular pan, then cut into bars or squares. Brownies are the best known.

3. *Rolled Cookies:* The dough is chilled, then rolled out thin with a rolling pin and cut with a cookie cutter or a knife. Although they are sometimes considered more trouble to prepare (you have to wait while the dough chills), rolled cookies are also handy: You can roll out just part of the dough, and keep the rest refrigerated (or frozen). That way, you can roll out and bake a few cookies in minutes, any time you want them freshly baked. Popular examples: sugar cookies, many holiday cookies.

4. *Refrigerator Cookies:* The dough is formed in cylindrical rolls and chilled (or frozen), then sliced and baked. Easy to do, and like rolled cookies (above), once you've got the dough on hand, you can slice and bake a few any time you like.

TECHNIQUES FOR PERFECT COOKIES

Before You Begin

- *Getting Started* Read through the recipe, making sure you have everything you'll need.
- *Take out the butter and eggs ahead* This brings them to room temperature for easy creaming. (And always use real butter.)
- *Get Organized* Assembling all your ingredients before you begin is a big help. The recipes in this book were written to make most efficient use of your time, so follow the instructions in order.
- *Preparing Cookie Sheets* Nonstick baking sheets work well for cookies (see page 21) as they don't need to be greased (or buttered and floured) at all. If the finish is slightly worn, rub the sheet with a light coating of butter or shortening. Regular baking sheets are fine, too—but avoid heavy black steel sheets, which can overbrown the bottoms before the cookies have baked through.
- *If You Don't Own Enough Baking Sheets* No problem. Just butter (or butter and flour, according to the recipe) a double thickness of aluminum foil for each sheet you need. Place or spoon the cookie dough on the foil. Then, once a cookie sheet is free, just slide the sheet carefully under the foil and bake as usual.

Mixing the Dough

- *Electric Mixer vs. Food Processor vs. Mixing by Hand*   Most of the recipes in this book are made in an electric mixer, which incorporates air as it creams butter and sugar, resulting in a light, fluffy dough—just what you want when making cookies. If you don't own a mixer, you can make most cookie doughs by hand, creaming the butter and sugar in a large mixing bowl with a wooden spoon, or in a food processor. The processor mixes cookie dough in seconds (don't overmix), but it doesn't aerate it as much.

- *Don't Rush Creaming the Butter and Sugar*   Take your time, and the mixture will become smooth and fluffy, giving you nice light cookies.

IF YOU FORGET TO TAKE OUT THE BUTTER BEFOREHAND . . .

- Just grate the cold butter into the mixing bowl, using the large holes of a standard grater. It will warm up quickly.
- Or do as French pastry chefs do: Cut the butter in pieces and place in a heatproof mixing bowl. Place the bowl on a stovetop burner, over low heat. Break the butter up with a wooden spoon until it becomes warm, soft, and creamy—but not melted (there will still be a few solid pieces). Now mix it in the electric mixer, and it should soon become fluffy.

- *Don't Overmix* any cookie dough once you add the flour. If you overwork the flour, you'll wind up with tough cookies.

- *Mixing Cookie Dough in Advance*   With most recipes, you can prepare cookie dough ahead. Cookie doughs that are rolled or sliced must be refrigerated, to firm them up for easy handling. They'll keep for 3 or 4 days tightly wrapped and refrigerated, 3 to 6 months frozen. But doughs for drop cookies are better made just before baking, so the dough doesn't dry out, or begin a chemical reaction caused by the baking powder. If you can't use a drop cookie dough immediately, refrigerate it as soon as possible in its bowl, tightly covered, for up to 1 day to slow down the chemical reaction of the baking powder.

- *Forming Cookies* While you don't want your cookies to look machine-made, try to get them as uniform in size as possible. Most recipes indicate how much dough to use for each cookie ("a rounded tablespoonful," etc.). You can make the cookies larger or smaller if you like, but you may have to adjust the baking time accordingly.

Baking

- *Baking Two Sheets at the Same Time* You can bake two cookie sheets at the same time, as long as the oven racks are spaced well apart, the sheets aren't directly over each other, and there is enough space for air to circulate between the edges of the cookie sheets and the oven walls. For even baking, it's usually a good idea to switch positions of the sheets themselves halfway through baking time.
- *For Even Baking* If your oven heats unevenly, try rotating the sheets (that is, turning them back to front) halfway through baking time.
- *When Are They Done?* Good question. Cookies bake quickly, so don't put them in the oven and leave the kitchen. Each of the recipes in this book will tell you what to look for in a properly baked cookie ("lightly browned around the edges," for example), as well as providing baking times, but please remember that *all baking times are approximate.* Set your timer for about 3 minutes *before* the baking time indicated; after the elapsed time, check the cookies carefully every minute or so. Just one minute more or less can be the difference between cookies that melt in your mouth, and cookies that are dry as dust. A general rule for all cookies: *Take care not to overbake.*

Cooling

- *Be Prepared* Set out cooling racks as soon as the cookies go into the oven. (If the cookies are especially crumbly, or if they're going to be iced, place the racks over sheets of wax paper for easy cleanup). Large, sturdy wire racks are best; they'll hold a big batch without crowding.

- *For Even Cooling*   Most cookies should be transferred to racks as soon as they come out of the oven, so they become crisp; otherwise the steam they emit as they cool will make them soggy. (Some recipes indicate otherwise, as for cookies that are too delicate to handle when just out of the oven; follow instructions for handling of these carefully.) Be sure to place them on the racks in a *single layer*.
- *Once Cooled Completely,* cookies can be overlapped to save space, or transferred to a platter, or to a cookie jar or tins for storage.

CAN I FREEZE COOKIES?

Many cookies can be frozen successfully; their flavor is at its best if kept no longer than 3 months.

- *Even Better:* Freeze the *unbaked* cookie dough (for rolled or sliced cookies) in small batches; then defrost and bake as many as you need. That way, any time you feel like making a quick batch of cookies, you can roll out a few, or slice them off a roll of dough, with (almost) no work. That way they'll always be freshly baked, and at their best.

Storing Cookies

- *Store Cookies Airtight* to preserve crispness. Keep a couple of tins with tight covers on hand. And cookie jars and cookies were "made for each other."
- *To Prevent Breakage,* place sheets of wax paper between each layer of cookies, as well as on the bottom and top of the tin.

TO RE-CRISP COOKIES . . .

If cookies get soft after standing for a day or so, just place them on a baking sheet and bake at 350°F. for 3 or 4 minutes to crisp them up again. Transfer to a wire rack to cool.

A FEW NOTES ON INGREDIENTS

THE COOKIE-LOVER'S PHILOSOPHY OF INGREDIENTS

Always use the finest ingredients you can get for homemade cookies.
Cookies are, by their very nature, special, and deserve the best.

None of the cookies in this book call for hard-to-find or unusual ingredients. But you'll have best results if you use the same ingredients that were used to test the recipes. Follow these guidelines:

Butter   Use *unsalted butter* for best flavor. If you'd like to substitute margarine for health reasons, go ahead. But if it's expense or calories you're concerned about, save on something else—nothing tastes like real butter in cookies. For greasing cookie sheets, either butter or solid vegetable shortening is fine.

Sugar   Means *granulated sugar.*

Brown Sugar   Most recipes specify light or dark brown sugar. If the type is not indicated, you can use either, or "Brownulated" (granular brown sugar). Don't substitute liquid brown sugar.

Flour   Means *unbleached all-purpose flour.* Don't sift unless directed to.

Cake Flour   Use *regular cake flour,* not self-rising. If you can't find cake flour, you can improvise by placing 2 tablespoons cornstarch in a 1-cup measure, then spooning in all-purpose flour until you have 1 level cup. This mixture can now be substituted for 1 cup cake flour.

MEASURE CAREFULLY . . .

All measurements in the recipes are *level.* With flour, spoon into the measuring cup, then level off. Always measure carefully; a little more or less can make a big difference in a cookie dough.

Eggs   All recipes were tested with eggs graded *"large."*

Lemon Juice   Means *freshly squeezed.*

GETTING THE MOST OUT OF LEMON (ORANGE, ETC.) ZEST . . .

In recipes that call for citrus zest (the colored part of the fruit's skin, with none of the bitter white pith underneath) it's best to add it when creaming the butter and sugar. The sugar acts as an abrasive, releasing the fragrant citrus oils found in the zest. This provides maximum fruit flavor.

Nuts   Buy nuts only from dealers you trust to carry fresh products because they can quickly become stale, or even rancid. (High turnover is a good indication.) To preserve freshness, *store nuts, tightly wrapped, in the freezer* (they don't need to be defrosted before you add them to a cookie dough).

Spices   If the ones on your shelf are more than a year old, replace them, because they aren't worth using unless they're *fresh.* If in doubt, smell them—if they're not fresh and fragrant, they're not going to contribute much to your cookies.

Vanilla   Use only *pure vanilla extract,* never imitation.

Chocolate   Varieties of chocolate are indicated in each recipe. Most brands work fine (Nestlés semisweet morsels can't be beat)—but for a real treat, buy some premium-quality chocolate, either imported or Van Leer American.

Cocoa   Use *unsweetened,* the best you can find.

Oatmeal   Use either *regular or "quick-cooking" oats*—not "instant oatmeal."

Coconut   Either *sweetened or unsweetened shredded coconut* can be used for these recipes.

Raisins and Dried Fruit   As with nuts, buy only where you trust that products are fresh. Choose *plump, moist dried fruit—not* glacéed fruit, which is preserved in a sugar syrup.

HOW TO CLEAN UP—FAST

1. *Clean As You Go*   An all-important rule, which prevents "after-baking panic." Put away each ingredient as soon as you finish with it, and cleaning up the kitchen will be a snap (well, almost).

2. *Place a Sheet of Wax Paper Under the Electric Mixer Before You Start.* Ingredients inevitably spatter, even when you're careful.

3. *Sift Dry Ingredients onto a Sheet of Wax Paper*   Then just throw it away after the ingredients have been added—nothing to wash. Some people also like to line the entire work surface with wax paper before they begin, to avoid messing up countertops.

4. *Once the Cookies Are in the Oven*   Place the mixing bowl in the sink as soon as you've finished with it. Squirt in some detergent, fill with hot water, and place all your utensils in the bowl. They'll soak clean in a few minutes, so they can be washed quickly (or put in the dishwasher). Then, when your cookies come out of the oven, you can enjoy them in a clean kitchen.

EQUIPMENT
A Few Things to Have on Hand for Cookie-Baking

While I'm not gadget crazy, here are some of my favorite useful items for cookie-baking:

- *KitchenAid Mixer*   It mixes energetically, and is beautiful to look at, too. The Kenwood mixer is also good, and hand mixers are fine for all but the heaviest doughs. You can also mix a cookie dough fairly quickly by hand, using a wooden spoon, a large mixing bowl, and some elbow grease.

- *Food Processor*   You'll notice that a processor is called for in a lot of these recipes, especially for cookie doughs that contain ground nuts. So many people now own food processors that they've become standard kitchen equipment. If you don't have one, an inexpensive Mouli grater grinds nuts to a fluffy powder by hand. (You can also use the processor to mix cookie doughs, but they won't become as fluffy.)

- *SilverStone-coated Baking Sheets*   These are *great* for cookies; invest in two or three. They don't need to be greased, though a light coating insures easy lift-off after baking. SilverStone-coated muffin tins save a lot of trouble, too. If you don't want nonstick

TIPS FOR MAILING COOKIES

Who wouldn't like to be surprised by a package of home-baked cookies in the mail? Just remember that you've got to take every precaution possible to avoid broken cookies (no one wants to get a package of crumbs!). Remember:

- Don't even *try* to mail cookies that are fragile.
- Some bar cookies, like brownies, stay fresher if wrapped individually in foil before packing them in tins.
- Choose sturdy, noncrushable tins with tight-fitting covers. A pretty tin makes your cookie gift extra-special.
- Insulate the tins with several layers of tissue paper on top and bottom, and with wax paper between layers of cookies. If you can get it, sheets of plastic bubble-pack (the kind everyone loves to pop) make an even better packing material. Line the mailing cartons with plenty of crumpled newspaper, also, to avoid jostling the tins.
- Mail cookies while still very fresh, and mark all cookie packages "Fragile."

---

sheets, get good, heavy-gauge ones—but not black steel. And be sure there is at least 1-inch clearance between the sheets and the oven walls for proper heat circulation.

- *Large, Sturdy Cooling Rack (with plenty of air space underneath)*   This is essential; without it, your cookies can get soggy. Available at department or cookware stores.
- *Large Rubber Spatula*   Professional-size spatulas clean out a bowl of cookie dough in a couple of quick strokes. Buy two or three; they're found in any good cookware shop.
- *Zester*   This handy stainless steel tool with several little holes grates lemon, orange, or lime zest quickly, without taking your knuckles with it. Chop the long strands of zest fine with a chef's knife after grating. If you don't have a zester, a vegetable peeler also removes zest in nice thin strips, which can then be chopped with a knife.
- *Dough Scraper (Bench Knife)*   Not strictly necessary, but lifts a whole batch of dough or a rolled-out sheet of pastry from a floured board, and scrapes the board clean afterward, too.

- *Spatulas*   A good, flat spatula is a must for lifting cookies from baking sheets. Get a plastic spatula if you use nonstick sheets.

Of course, a good chef's knife is a must in any kitchen, as are a sharp vegetable peeler, 8- and 9-inch square baking pans, and other basics.

COOKIES THAT DON'T CRUMBLE—THE BEST COOKIES FOR MAILING

Any of the following are good choices for mailing:

- All Cookie Jar Cookies (except Maida Heatter's Oatmeal Wafers), pages 28–37
- Iced Spice Snaps, page 46
- Black & White Butter Pretzels, page 52
- Kitchen Sink Granola Bars, page 53
- Chocolate-Dipped Peanut Brittle Fingers, page 54
- Chunky White Chocolate–Macadamia Cookies, page 64
- Coconut-Chip Blondies, page 66
- Disappearing Double Chocolate Brownies, page 68
- Milk Chocolate–Toasted Almond Candy Bar Cookies, page 70
- Mary's Fruit Rolls, page 76
- Baby Fruitcakes, page 90
- Grandma's Mohn Moons, page 104
- Toasted Sesame Biscuits, page 105
- Chocolate-Dipped Hazelnut Shortbread Wedges, page 119
- Anisette Toasts, page 126
- Chocolate-Glazed Lebkuchen, page 128
- Portuguese Almond Macaroons, page 130
- Swedish Dream Cookies, page 134
- Greek Almond Crescents (Kourambiedes), page 135

YOUR BASIC COOKIE JAR COOKIES
Which No Home
Should Be Without

Butterscotch Crunch Cookies
Old-Time Coconut Jumbles
Gingerbread Hermits
Nancy's Wonderful Sour Cream Cookies *and* Cocoa Drops
Iced Applesauce Raisin Cookies
Carlo's Sugar Diamonds
Date Chewies with Sour Cream
Praline Snowcaps
Ruth's Chewy Granola Cookies
Pumpkin Munchies
Maida Heatter's Oatmeal Wafers
Other Cookie Jar Cookies

When we were young, a full cookie jar, with cookies nestled tantalizingly inside, meant having more than just cookies. It meant that someone—Mom, Grandma, a friend, whoever—was there, caring about us. We knew that whenever we needed it, a comforting bite (whether soft or crunchy) was just a reach away. And we felt nourished, in ways both physical and more essential.

But there came a time when we had to grow up and move beyond depending only on the care of others. That doesn't mean, however, giving up forever the pleasures of having a cookie jar around. In fact, when you're on your own, it's even more important to keep your cookie jar full—ready to be visited whenever you need to treat yourself or lift your spirits. And that sometimes means providing them for yourself, by yourself.

Here's a collection of nice-to-have-around-the-house cookies. They're homey (not elegant) and keep well, so you can always have some on hand.

BUTTERSCOTCH CRUNCH COOKIES

A real cookie jar cookie, with melt-in-your-mouth butterscotch flavor.

Makes about 30 cookies, 3 inches in diameter

½ **cup (1 stick) unsalted butter, softened**
1 **cup dark brown sugar**
1 **egg**
2 **teaspoons pure vanilla extract**
1¼ **cups flour**
1 **teaspoon baking powder**
½ **teaspoon baking soda**
¼ **teaspoon cinnamon**
⅛ **teaspoon salt**
1 **cup coarsely chopped pecans (or walnuts)**

1. Preheat the oven to 375°F. Butter two baking sheets; set aside.

2. Cream the butter and brown sugar in an electric mixer at medium speed until light, about 3 minutes. Add the egg and vanilla; continue to beat until the mixture is smooth. Meanwhile, sift the flour, baking powder, baking soda, cinnamon, and salt onto a sheet of wax paper. Lower the mixer speed and add the dry ingredients, mixing just until blended. Stir in the pecans.

3. Drop the dough by level tablespoonfuls onto the baking sheets, spacing them 2 inches apart (these cookies spread as they bake). Bake 8 minutes. Let the cookies cool for a few minutes on the baking sheets to firm up; then transfer to a wire rack to cool completely. Store airtight, with wax paper between layers. These cookies keep well for several days, and also make good gifts.

OLD-TIME COCONUT JUMBLES

Jumbles are a very old cookie, mentioned in lots of early American cookbooks. This particular version is based on an 1825 recipe for "Jumbals" in Mary Randolph's *The Virginia Housewife* (University of South Carolina Press). Food historian Karen Hess notes that their name derives from European versions of the cookie—the Italian *ciambelline* and the French *gimblettes*. Usually, the dough was rolled out and cut into thin strips, which were then twisted in knotted forms, such as pretzels or figure eights. Later, ring shapes were more common. The Jumbles in this recipe are simple buttery rounds, topped with coconut, which toasts gently as the cookies bake.

Makes 2 to 3 dozen

1 cup (2 sticks) unsalted butter, softened
1 cup sugar
½ teaspoon pure vanilla extract
2 drops almond extract
2 eggs
2 cups flour
2 cups shredded coconut, sweetened or unsweetened
¼ teaspoon nutmeg, preferably grated fresh
1 egg white, lightly beaten

1. Cream the butter and the sugar in an electric mixer at medium speed until very light, 3 to 5 minutes. Add the vanilla and almond extracts, then the eggs, one at a time. Lower the speed and add the flour, 1 cup of the coconut, and nutmeg, mixing just until well blended, no longer. Chill overnight, or at least 2 hours.

2. Preheat the oven to 350°F. Lightly butter four baking sheets (or sheets of aluminum foil). Divide the dough in quarters. Place one portion of dough on a lightly floured surface, keeping the remainder refrigerated. Roll out the dough to a thickness of ⅜ inch. Cut out 3- to 3½-inch circles with a fluted or plain cookie cutter dipped in flour. Place the cookies on the baking sheets, spacing them about 1 inch apart. Repeat with remaining dough, and reroll chilled scraps.

3. Brush the cookies with a light coating of egg white; then sprinkle them with the remaining coconut, dividing it evenly. Bake until the edges are lightly golden, about 11 minutes. Transfer to a wire rack to cool completely; then store.

GINGERBREAD HERMITS

An old-time soft bar cookie, based on a Rhode Island recipe from my friend Mary Codola. They remind me of the bakery in the small town where I grew up, which baked only a few kinds of cookies, but each one was special. The hermits were my favorite—moist, chewy, and with plenty of raisins and spices. And Mary's are even better.

Makes about 4½ dozen

1 cup (2 sticks) unsalted butter, softened
2½ cups light brown sugar (slightly over 1 pound)
4 eggs
⅓ cup molasses
4 cups flour
1½ teaspoons baking powder
1½ teaspoons baking soda
1½ teaspoons cinnamon
1 teaspoon ground ginger
1 teaspoon nutmeg, preferably grated fresh
¼ teaspoon ground cloves
½ teaspoon salt
3 tablespoons crystallized ginger, chopped fine
1 cup raisins
1 cup coarse-chopped walnuts or pecans

1. Preheat the oven to 375°F. Butter and flour three baking sheets (or sheets of foil); set aside.

2. Beat the butter in an electric mixer at medium speed; then add the brown sugar and cream the mixture until light, about 3 minutes. Add 3 of the eggs, one at a time, then the molasses, beating until smooth.

3. Meanwhile, sift the flour, baking powder, baking soda, cinnamon, ground ginger, nutmeg, cloves, and salt onto a sheet of wax paper. Lower the mixer speed and beat in the dry mixture just until blended. Add the crystallized ginger, raisins, and nuts; do not overmix.

4. With your fingers, form the dough into six "logs," two on each baking sheet. Make the log shapes as long as the baking sheets, and about 1 inch high and 1½ inches wide, spacing them well apart, as they will spread as they bake. Beat the remaining egg; brush the logs lightly with beaten egg.

5. Bake the hermits on the center rack of the oven until golden, but still quite soft. Check carefully; timing can vary from 10 to 14 minutes, but these cookies should not be overbaked. Place the baking sheets on a wire rack to cool; then slice the logs into bars 2 inches wide and store airtight. Hermits keep well for several days.

NANCY'S WONDERFUL SOUR CREAM COOKIES

These are my favorite basic soft cookies—the old-fashioned touch of combining baking soda with liquid makes them very light, like puffy little butter cakes. This recipe is from Nancy Hubbard in Indiana, whose family eats cookies just as fast as she can bake them—and she bakes plenty. For slightly more "adult" cookies, replace 1 tablespoon of the milk in the icing with a tablespoon of brandy or rum.

Makes about 4 dozen 2½-inch cookies

11 tablespoons (1 stick plus 3 tablespoons) unsalted butter, softened
1⅓ cups sugar
2 eggs
1 teaspoon pure vanilla extract
3 drops almond extract
⅔ cup sour cream
¾ teaspoon baking soda
2⅔ cups flour

VANILLA ICING:

1⅓ cups sifted confectioners' sugar
3 tablespoons milk
¾ teaspoon pure vanilla extract

1. Preheat the oven to 350°F. Butter three baking sheets (or sheets of foil); set aside.

2. In an electric mixer, cream the butter and sugar at medium speed until light, about 3 minutes. Add the eggs one at a time, then the vanilla and almond extracts. In a small bowl, stir together the sour cream and baking soda (the mixture will froth a little). Add the flour to the butter mixture alternately with the sour cream, beginning and ending with flour. Do not overmix.

3. Drop level tablespoonfuls of the dough onto the baking sheets, spacing them about an inch apart. Bake until lightly browned around the edges, 10 to 12 minutes. Transfer to a wire rack to cool slightly.

4. VANILLA ICING: In a small bowl, stir together the confectioners' sugar, milk, and vanilla until smooth. Brush the cookies with the icing while are still slightly warm; then cool until the icing has set.

Variation: Cocoa Drops
   For soft, light cookies with rich, rich flavor, reduce the flour to 2 cups; sift the flour with ⅔ cup unsweetened cocoa powder (in Step 2), and proceed with recipe. After icing, dust the cookies with cocoa through a fine strainer.

ICED APPLESAUCE RAISIN COOKIES

An all-American cookie—soft, large, and spicy. These cookies fill the house with a wonderful aroma as they bake. For best flavor, use homemade applesauce, made with either no sugar, or very little.

Makes about 3 dozen 3-inch cookies

½ **cup (1 stick) unsalted butter, softened**
⅓ **cup brown sugar**
¼ **cup granulated sugar**
1 **egg**
1 **cup applesauce, preferably unsweetened homemade**
1 **teaspoon pure vanilla extract**
2 **cups sifted flour**
½ **teaspoon baking powder**
½ **teaspoon baking soda**
¼ **teaspoon salt**
1 **teaspoon nutmeg, preferably grated fresh**
½ **teaspoon cinnamon**
½ **teaspoon ground allspice**
1 **cup raisins or currants**
1 **cup walnuts, chopped very coarse**

CRISSCROSS ICING:

2 **cups sifted confectioners' sugar**
2 **tablespoons milk, plus more as needed**
1 **teaspoon pure vanilla extract**

1. Preheat the oven to 350°F. Butter three baking sheets (or sheets of foil); set aside.

2. In an electric mixer, cream the butter and sugars at medium speed until light, about 3 minutes. Add the egg, then the applesauce and vanilla, mixing until smooth. Meanwhile, sift the flour, baking powder, baking soda, salt, nutmeg, cinnamon, and allspice onto a sheet of wax paper. Lower the mixer speed and add the flour mixture to the creamed mixture, mixing just until smooth, no longer. Mix in the raisins and walnuts; do not overmix.

3. Drop heaping tablespoonfuls of the dough onto the baking sheets, spacing them about 2 inches apart. With the back of a large spoon, spread the batter into flat 2½-inch rounds. Bake until browned around the edges, 12 to 13 minutes. Transfer the cookies to a wire rack set over a sheet of wax paper; cool completely.

4. CRISSCROSS ICING: In a small bowl, stir together the confectioners' sugar, milk, and vanilla until smooth. Test the consistency: The icing should be fluid, but should hold a line when drizzled from a fork onto a sheet of wax paper. Thin, if necessary, with a little more milk, adding a few drops at a time; if too thin, sift in a little more confectioners' sugar. Drizzle the icing back and forth over the cookies in thin lines. Let the cookies stand until the icing has set.

CARLO'S SUGAR DIAMONDS

This vanilla and orange-scented cookie dough comes from my former baking teacher, Carlo Bussetti. It's a good, all-purpose dough that makes a richly flavored base for bar cookies, or crisp tartlet shells. Make an extra batch; this dough freezes well.

Note: Pearl sugar is a large-grain sugar, available at cake decorating and food specialty shops. It can be ordered by mail from Paprikas Weiss, 1546 Second Avenue, New York, NY 10028 (telephone 212-288-6117). Send $1 for catalog.

Makes about 30 cookies

CARLO'S COOKIE DOUGH:

- 1 **cup (2 sticks) unsalted butter, softened**
- 1 **cup sugar**
  Pinch of salt
  Grated zest of 2 oranges
- ¼ **cup lightly beaten egg (1 large egg plus 1 yolk, or 1 extra-large egg)**
- 2 **tablespoons milk**
- 1 **tablespoon pure vanilla extract**
- 2 **cups cake flour (6 ounces)**
- 1½ **cup all-purpose flour (6 ounces)**

SUGAR GLAZE:

- 1 **egg white, lightly beaten**
  Pearl sugar (or substitute granulated sugar)

1. **CARLO'S COOKIE DOUGH:** Beat the butter in an electric mixer at medium speed until light. Gradually add the sugar; then add the salt and orange zest and cream the mixture until very fluffy. Beat in the egg, milk, and vanilla. Lower the mixer speed and add both flours, mixing just until incorporated, no longer. The dough should be soft, but not sticky. Gather the dough together on a sheet of plastic wrap lightly sprinkled with flour. Wrap tight and chill well, at least 2 hours. Soften briefly at room temperature before rolling out.

2. Preheat the oven to 350°F. Lightly grease two baking sheets. Roll the dough on a lightly floured surface to a neat 10 × 12-inch rectangle about ¼ inch thick. Brush the dough lightly with the egg white; then sprinkle with a light but even coating of pearl sugar. With a fluted pastry wheel, cut across the width in a series of parallel lines spaced about 2 inches apart. Cut across the parallel lines at a sharp diagonal, forming neat diamond shapes (the scraps can be rerolled).

3. Carefully transfer the diamonds with a spatula to the baking sheets and bake until lightly golden, 15 to 18 minutes. Transfer to a wire rack to cool; store airtight.

DATE CHEWIES WITH SOUR CREAM

These cookie jar cookies are based on recipes for Billy Goats, which are old favorites in California, and also in the South.

Makes about 40 cookies, 3 inches in diameter

½ cup (1 stick) unsalted butter, softened
1 cup sugar
2 eggs
½ cup sour cream
1 cup all-purpose flour
1 cup whole wheat flour
2 teaspoons baking powder
½ teaspoon baking soda
1 teaspoon ground allspice
1 cup chopped walnuts
2 cups chopped pitted dates (1 pound)

1. Preheat the oven to 350°F. Butter two cookie sheets; set aside.

2. Cream the butter and sugar in an electric mixer at medium speed until light, about 3 minutes. Add the eggs, one at a time, and then the sour cream, beating until the mixture is smooth.

3. Meanwhile, sift together both flours, the baking powder, baking soda, and allspice on a sheet of wax paper. Lower the mixer speed and gradually add the dry mixture to the butter until blended; do not overbeat. Stir in the walnuts and the dates.

4. Drop the mixture by rounded tablespoonfuls onto the cookie sheets, spacing them 1½ inches apart. Bake until lightly browned, 15 to 17 minutes. Transfer the cookies to a wire rack to cool. Cool completely before storing in an airtight container, with wax paper between the layers.

PRALINE SNOWCAPS

Crisp meringue kisses, with the dusky flavors of brown sugar, pecans, and toasted coconut. My friend chef Ruth Cousineau felt a burst of nostalgia when she bit into these while testing—her mother used to bake similar cookies for her with cornflakes and walnuts, and they were her childhood favorite.

Makes 4 dozen

2 **cups shredded coconut**
1½ **cups coarsely broken pecans**
4 **egg whites**
   Pinch of salt
1 **cup light brown sugar**
1 **teaspoon pure vanilla extract**

1. Preheat the oven to 300°F. Place the coconut and pecans on a baking sheet and toast until lightly golden, 8 to 10 minutes (watch carefully). Remove from the oven and cool slightly; lower the oven heat to 250°F., with two racks evenly spaced in the oven. Lightly grease two baking sheets; set aside.

2. In an electric mixer, beat the egg whites and salt at medium speed until they nearly form soft peaks. Raise the mixer speed slightly and add the brown sugar, a tablespoon at a time, beating constantly until the meringue forms stiff peaks but is still glossy, 5 to 8 minutes. With a large rubber spatula, gently fold the vanilla, coconut, and pecans into the meringue.

3. Spoon the mixture by rounded tablespoonfuls onto the baking sheets, spacing them about an inch apart. Bake until the outsides of the cookies are dry to the touch, 45 to 50 minutes. (Exchange the positions of the pans halfway through if the cookies are baking unevenly.)

4. Place the baking pans on a wire rack and cool the cookies on the pans. When cool, carefully remove cookies from the pans with a spatula. Store these cookies airtight.

RUTH'S CHEWY GRANOLA COOKIES

These are what cookies are all about—crisp outside, chewy within, not too sweet, with lots of flavor. And as you eat them by the handful, you can remind yourself that the bran and granola are good for you. From chef Ruth Cousineau.

Makes about 32 cookies, 3 inches in diameter

½ cup (1 stick) butter, softened
1 cup (packed) brown sugar
1 egg
1½ cups granola
1 cup whole wheat flour
½ cup unprocessed bran
1 teaspoon cinnamon
1 teaspoon baking powder
½ teaspoon baking soda
¼ teaspoon salt
1 cup golden raisins

1. Preheat the oven to 400°F. Butter two baking sheets; set aside.

2. Cream the butter and sugar in an electric mixer at medium speed until light, about 3 minutes. Add the egg and continue to beat until the mixture is smooth. Meanwhile, mix together the dry ingredients: granola, whole wheat flour, bran, cinnamon, baking powder, baking soda, and salt. Add this mixture, then the raisins, to the butter, mixing until blended.

3. Drop the dough by rounded tablespoonfuls onto the baking sheets, spacing them 2 inches apart (these cookies spread as they bake). Bake until golden brown, 10 to 12 minutes. Transfer to a wire rack to cool. Cool the cookies completely before storing airtight, with wax paper between layers. These cookies keep well for several days, and can also be mailed as gifts.

PUMPKIN MUNCHIES

Like soft little cakes—just right for Halloween. If you like, these can be glazed with a thin icing (such as the Vanilla Icing on p. 31).

Makes about 2½ dozen 2½-inch cookies

½ cup chopped dried apricots
½ cup dried currants or raisins
¼ cup bourbon or rum (or apple cider)
½ cup (1 stick) unsalted butter, softened
½ cup light brown sugar
¼ cup honey
1 egg
1 cup mashed pumpkin, fresh (see Note below) or canned unsweetened
1 teaspoon pure vanilla extract
2 cups flour
1 teaspoon baking powder
½ teaspoon baking soda
¼ teaspoon salt
1 teaspoon nutmeg, preferably grated fresh
½ teaspoon cinnamon
½ teaspoon ground allspice
   Large pinch of fresh-ground pepper
1 cup coarse-chopped walnuts or pecans

1. Soak the apricots and currants in the bourbon or cider and let stand, stirring once or twice, while you make the cookie dough.

2. Preheat the oven to 375°F. Butter two baking sheets; set aside.

3. In an electric mixer at medium speed, cream the butter with the sugar and honey until light, about 3 minutes. Add the egg, then the mashed pumpkin and vanilla, beating until smooth.

4. Meanwhile, sift the flour onto a sheet of wax paper with the baking powder, baking soda, salt, nutmeg, cinnamon, allspice, and pepper. Lower the mixer speed and add the dry mixture, mixing just until blended, no longer. Stir in the dried fruits (and any soaking liquid) and the nuts.

5. Spoon the dough onto the baking sheets by heaping tablespoonfuls, spacing them about 1 inch apart. Bake until lightly golden, 12 to 14 minutes. Transfer to a wire rack to cool; then store.

Note: To prepare mashed fresh pumpkin, break off the stem of any size pumpkin, then cut pumpkin in half crosswise and scoop out seeds and stringy interior. Place pumpkin, cut sides down, on a foil-lined baking sheet, cover with foil, and bake at 350°F. until the flesh is very tender, about 1½ hours. Cool, then scoop out flesh and mash with a potato masher or purée in a food processor. If the mashed pumpkin is watery, drain in a cheesecloth-lined colander or sieve before using.

MAIDA HEATTER'S OATMEAL WAFERS

Very crisp! Heavy on the Nutmeg But Good!

I've made these crisp, delicious wafers so many times that they've become a standard at my house. As their creator explains, they shouldn't be stored in cookie jars, because they're *extremely* fragile—*Handle with Care!* Even so, they are so full of good old-fashioned oatmeal-spice flavor that they belong in this chapter.

Maida Heatter needs no introduction, of course. She's America's best-loved dessert authority, and she's especially fond of cookies. "Almost always," Maida says, "when I need a quick, or not so quick, gift for someone, my first thought is cookies."

12 cookies per sheet covered with foil. (3 sheets)

Makes about 30 cookies

¼ **cup sifted flour**
½ **teaspoon salt**
⅛ **teaspoon baking soda**
½ **teaspoon cinnamon**
½ **teaspoon ground cloves**
½ **teaspoon allspice**
½ **teaspoon powdered ginger**
½ **teaspoon nutmeg, preferably grated fresh**
½ **cup (1 stick) unsalted butter, softened**
1 **teaspoon pure vanilla extract**
½ **cup light brown sugar, packed firm**
¼ **cup granulated sugar**
1 **egg**
1 **cup regular or quick-cooking oats (not instant oatmeal)**
½ **cup walnuts, chopped medium-fine**

1. Adjust a rack one-third down from the top of the oven and preheat to 350°F. Cut aluminum foil to fit three cookie sheets.

2. Resift the flour with the salt, baking soda, cinnamon, cloves, allspice, ginger, and nutmeg. Set aside.

3. Cream the butter in the small bowl of an electric mixer. Add the vanilla and both sugars and beat for a minute or two. Beat in the egg and then the oatmeal. On lowest speed, add the sifted dry ingredients and then the nuts, scraping the bowl with a rubber spatula and beating until well mixed.

4. Drop the batter on the foil-lined baking sheets (or just the foil, if you don't own 3 sheets) by slightly rounded teaspoonfuls, placing them far apart —about 3 inches—as they spread a lot. With the back of a teaspoon dipped repeatedly in cold water, spread each cookie to flatten it. Make it thin, but don't worry about keeping the shape round.

5. Bake about 15 minutes until completely browned, reversing the position of the cookie sheet,

back to front during baking to insure even browning. Slide the aluminum foil off the cookie sheet. Bake remaining cookies, sliding cookie sheets under the full sheets of foil as necessary. Allow to cool completely on the foil and then peel the foil away from the backs of the cookies.

6. Place the cookies on a platter or tray and cover airtight with plastic wrap. The wafers must be stored airtight, and may be frozen.

Other Cookie Jar Cookies:

GREAT MOMENTS IN COOKIE HISTORY: PART ONE

? B.C. Earliest cookies on record, small cakes used in sacrifices by the Egyptians. These cakes were imprinted with horns to symbolize an ox, or cut in the shape of a man, and substituted for live sacrifices to the gods. Germanic tribes often followed the same practice in times of poverty, when an ox could not be spared. These imprinted cookies were early versions of the popular German *Springerle* wafers.

? B.C. Assyrians, Babylonians, and Greeks use small, cookielike cakes in religious ceremonies. The Greeks called their mixture of fine flour and honey *bouen*—which later became the word "bun."

17th century Gingerbread becomes popular, first made with breadcrumbs and honey, and later molasses, a new by-product of refined sugar. These cookies are frequently flavored with pepper, as the spices ginger and pepper were often used together in medieval recipes.

1730 Earliest mention in the Oxford English Dictionary of the word "cookie," in a Scottish reference to Dutch *koekje* (cookies)—a diminutive of *koek* (cake).

1796 Publication of the first American cookbook, *American Cookery* by Amelia Simmons, "Orphan." Simmons includes a recipe for "Cookies" flavored with coriander seed, and leavened with pearl ash dissolved in milk. Also a recipe for a "Christmas Cookey," which, she advises, "tho' hard and dry at first, if put into an earthen pot, and dry cellar, or damp room, they will be finer, softer and better when six months old."

Gail Weesner, editor of the 1982 edition of *American Cookery* (Rowan Tree Press, Boston), notes that "To this day 'cookie' is an Americanism; in England it is a biscuit, or simply a small cake. The American term probably came out of the contact of the English settlers with the descendants of the Dutch of New Amsterdam [New York]."

1808   Washington Irving's *Salmagundi* mentions "those notable cakes . . . cookies."

1870s   Wood-burning iron ranges appear, whose even heat make it feasible to bake cookies at home. Up to the Civil War, housewives were still cooking in fireplaces. Coal-burning stoves appeared slightly later, at about the turn of the 20th century.

1902   Nabisco introduces Barnum's Animal Crackers, one of its all-time best-selling cookies.

1908   Hydrox Cookies, an all-American classic, are introduced by Sunshine Biscuits. In its search for a name for its sandwich cookie, Sunshine was inspired by water, "because water and sunshine are elements of purity and cleanliness." Water being a combination of *hydr*ogen and *ox*ygen, the name Hydrox was born— and so was Sunshine's most popular cookie.

1912 (March 6)   Nabisco introduces Oreo sandwich cookies. Lorna Doone appeared a week later, probably named for the heroine of a 19th-century Scottish romance by R. D. Blackmore. Many Nabisco cookies go even further back; Premium crackers have been around since 1876.

1914 (?)   First recipe for brownies. The folks at Betty Crocker say that they may have been "invented" accidentally when a chocolate cake fell. Maida Heatter reports that she may have found a clue to the origin of brownies from Mrs. "Brownie" Schrumpf, an octogenarian who is a local food authority at the Maine Historical Society in Bangor, Maine. Mrs. Schrumpf remembers a cookbook published by the local YWCA in 1914, with a recipe for brownies. "That," according to Maida Heatter, "might have been the first brownie recipe in print."

GOOD-TIME COOKIES
As Much Fun to
Make as to Eat

Iced Spice Snaps
Happy Face Sugar Cookies
Lemon Piglets, Lions, and Sheep
Black & White Butter Pretzels
Kitchen Sink Granola Bars
Chocolate-Dipped Peanut Brittle Fingers
Giant Stacked Cookie Cake

Baking cookies is a fun way for parents and kids (or kids and kids) to spend time together. Plan a decorate-your-own-cookie party—set out decorations (see page 48 for suggestions), and let the kids go crazy.

Making cookies for holiday tree ornaments will also keep you warm inside on a cold afternoon. Be sure to make a few extra—once you've finished baking, you'll get to enjoy the products of your hard work.

ICED SPICE SNAPS

These look good when cut with a star-shaped cookie cutter, or use any cutter you like (I like one in the shape of a small hand). This is an old recipe, very fragrant, with pepper and vinegar for deep flavor (note that the dough has to be prepared a day in advance). It's an easy dough to roll out, and the cookies become even more fragrant as they keep. If you'd like to use these as tree ornaments, cut a small hole in the top of each cookie by pushing a small skewer through each one, about ½ inch from the top edge, as soon as you take them out of the oven.

Makes 4 dozen 3-inch cookies

2½ **cups flour**
  1 **teaspoon baking soda**
  1 **teaspoon cinnamon**
  1 **teaspoon ground ginger**
  ¼ **teaspoon ground cloves**
  ½ **teaspoon fresh-ground black pepper**
  ½ **cup (1 stick) unsalted butter, cut in pieces**
  ½ **cup dark brown sugar**
  ½ **cup molasses**
  2 **teaspoons cider vinegar**
  1 **egg yolk**

NUTMEG ICING:

  1 **cup sifted confectioners' sugar**
1½ **tablespoons milk**
  1 **tablespoon brandy (or another tablespoon milk)**
  ¼ **teaspoon nutmeg, preferably grated fresh**

1. Sift the flour, baking soda, cinnamon, ginger, cloves, and pepper into a mixing bowl. Set aside.

2. Melt the butter in a heavy saucepan with the brown sugar, molasses, and vinegar, stirring until the sugar has dissolved. Stir this mixture into the flour mixture, then add the egg yolk and stir until the dough is well blended (the dough will be very sticky). Cool the dough to room temperature; then transfer the dough to a sheet of plastic wrap, wrap tight, and refrigerate overnight.

3. Preheat the oven to 350°F. Butter two or three baking sheets (or sheets of aluminum foil); set aside. Divide the dough in half. Place one portion of dough on a lightly floured surface, keeping the remainder refrigerated. Roll out the dough to a thickness of ⅛ inch. With floured cookie cutters, cut out stars, hands, and other fanciful shapes. With a spatula, transfer the cookies to the baking sheets. Repeat with remaining dough, and reroll chilled scraps. If the dough becomes soft, chill briefly, right on the baking sheets.

4. Bake until set and dry to the touch (the edges will be barely colored, but it's hard to tell because the dough is brown already), 7 to 8 minutes. Don't

overbake; these cookies are quite thin, and the molasses can scorch easily. (If you'd like to poke holes in the cookies with a skewer, so they can be hung from a tree, do it now.) Transfer to a wire rack to cool.

5. **NUTMEG ICING:** In a small bowl, stir together the confectioners' sugar, milk, brandy, and nutmeg until smooth. Brush the cookies with the icing when they have thoroughly cooled. Let stand until the icing has set.

A DECORATE-YOUR-OWN-COOKIE PARTY

Iced Spice Snaps are perfect for a kids' party. Let each guest trace his or her own hand in the spicy dough, and once you've set out the trimmings, the children can decorate the cookies as they like. Other good doughs for decorating are the Lemon–Cream Cheese Dough and the Happy Face dough (pages 50 and 49).

Have on Hand for Decorating:

- Red and black licorice "whips"
- M & M's, or "Reese's Pieces"
- Semisweet chocolate morsels
- Gumdrops or jelly beans
- Slices of marshmallow
- Cinnamon drops
- Melted chocolate
- Small paint brushes

Decorating the Cookies: After the cookies are baked, the fun begins. Each child decorates his or her own hand cookie, designing it as he or she likes. The cookies should be iced before decorating. A few tips:

- Decorations should be pressed into the icing while it is still wet. For a white matte finish, ice the cookies after they have cooled completely.
- Some items, like a slice of marshmallow for the face of a watch, will have to be fastened to the surface of the cookie, using the icing as "glue."
- Once the cookies are decorated, let them stand on a wire rack until the icing and decorations have set.

Here are just a few possibilities for decorating the cookies:

- a bracelet of licorice "whip," with M & M or gumdrop "charms"
- painted fingernails, using M & M's, jelly beans, or gumdrops
- a glove, painted with icing, trimmed with candies
- a watch—use a slice of (large) marshmallow as the face, licorice as the watchband, and 4 red cinnamon candies to indicate 4 numbers. The hands can be thin strips of licorice, or can be painted on, using a small brush dipped in melted chocolate.
- Kids can ice the cookies, then write their own names, using a small brush dipped in melted chocolate.

HAPPY FACE SUGAR COOKIES

Big sugar cookies—simple, rich and buttery. Kids can experiment with these, creating whatever expressions they like on the faces.

Makes about 20 cookies, 4 inches in diameter

1 cup (2 sticks) unsalted butter, softened
1 cup sugar
2 teaspoons pure vanilla extract
3 or 4 drops almond extract
2 eggs
2 cups flour

1. In an electric mixer, cream the butter and the sugar at medium speed until very light, 3 to 5 minutes. Add the vanilla and almond extracts, then the eggs, one at a time. Lower the mixer speed and add the flour, mixing just until well blended, no longer. Chill until the dough is firm—overnight, or at least 2 hours.

2. Preheat the oven to 350°F. Lightly butter four baking sheets or sheets of aluminum foil; set aside.

3. Divide the dough in quarters. Place one portion of dough on a lightly floured surface, keeping the remainder refrigerated. Roll out the dough to a thickness of ¼ inch. Cut out 3½- to 4-inch circles with a fluted or plain cookie cutter dipped in flour (or use a small saucer as a guide). Place the cookies on the baking sheets, spacing them about 1 inch apart.

4. Use a small round cutter (about ½ inch) or an apple corer or similar round implement to cut out two eyes in each face. With a crescent-shape cutter, cut out a smile (you can also do this with a small paring knife). Repeat with remaining dough, and with rerolled chilled scraps.

5. Bake the cookies until the edges are lightly golden, 10 to 11 minutes. Transfer to a wire rack to cool completely; then store airtight.

LEMON PIGLETS, LIONS AND SHEEP

This is such a good basic dough, easy to roll out, and rich with the "cheesecake" flavors of lemon and cream cheese, that it shouldn't be saved only for children's parties. But it is ideal for creating animals with distinctive touches: Pressing the dough through a (well-washed) garlic press creates "lions' manes" and "sheep's wool." (An alternative: Kids can cut out faces, using the garlic press to make "hair," and candies, as suggested for the Cookie Party on page 48, for eyes, etc.) For non-animal cookies, knead ¼ cup dried currants into the dough after removing it from the food processor in Step 1, and cut out shells, rounds, or any other simple shapes.

Note: Pearl sugar, used to decorate these cookies, is a large-grain sugar, available at cake decorating and food specialty shops; see page 33 for mail-order information.

Makes about 30 cookies

LEMON–CREAM CHEESE DOUGH:

Zest of 1 large lemon, removed in strips with a vegetable peeler
½ **cup sugar**
10 **tablespoons (1 stick plus 2 tablespoons) unsalted butter, softened**
3 **ounces (1 small package) cream cheese, softened**
3 **tablespoons fresh lemon juice**
2¼ **cups flour**
¼ **teaspoon salt**

1. **LEMON–CREAM CHEESE DOUGH:** In a food processor, process the lemon zest and sugar until the zest is finely chopped. Add the butter and cream cheese and mix until well blended and light. (*Note:* If using an electric mixer, grate the lemon zest first; then cream together sugar, lemon zest, butter, and cream cheese.) Add the lemon juice, flour, and salt, processing just until well combined, no longer. Place the dough on a lightly floured sheet of plastic wrap, wrap tight, and chill until firm, at least 2 hours.

2. Preheat the oven to 350°F. Lightly butter two or three baking sheets (or sheets of aluminum foil); set aside. Divide the dough in half; place half on a lightly floured surface, keeping the remainder refrigerated. Roll the dough to a thickness of ⅛ inch. Dip a pig-shape cookie cutter (or a lion, sheep, or any other cutter you like) in flour and cut out cookies, transferring them with a spatula to the baking sheets. Repeat with remaining dough, reserving the scraps.

GLAZE:

1 egg white
2 teaspoons fresh lemon juice
2 tablespoons pearl or
   granulated sugar
   Dried currants (raisins can be
   substituted)

3. GLAZE: Stir together the egg white and 2 teaspoons lemon juice with a fork. Brush the cookies with a light coating of this mixture; then sprinkle them with a light, even coating of pearl or granulated sugar. Now press a currant "eye" in each animal cookie.

4. DECORATION: Chill all dough scraps. For piglet tails, roll small pieces of the dough into small ropes about 4 inches long and ⅛ inch thick. Twist into a curlicue and fasten to the pigs, laying about half of the twisted tail on the surface of the pig, with half extending onto the cookie sheet. Lion tails can be made in the same way, using slightly less dough, and forming a curved tail (as described, half on the cookie, half extending onto the sheet—but don't form a curlicue.)

For lions or sheep, press the dough scraps through a clean garlic press, letting them fall loosely onto a sheet of wax paper. Pick up small piles of the strands of dough with a table knife and form a lion's mane on each lion cookie, plus a tuft of fur at the end of the tail. Press the strands very gently into the cookies without crushing them, so they stay in place. For sheep, lay "wool" along the length of the back of each sheep.

5. Bake the cookies until set and barely colored, about 10 minutes. (Don't let the insides of the cookies become completely dry—cut into one to check, if necessary.) Transfer to a wire rack until cool; then store. (Be very careful to prevent breaking the tails.)

BLACK & WHITE BUTTER PRETZELS

A rich cream cheese dough, formed into pretzels and dipped halfway in semisweet chocolate. For a mock salt effect, brush the unbaked pretzels with lightly beaten egg white and sprinkle with pearl sugar (page 33).

Makes 40 pretzels

½ cup (1 stick) unsalted butter, softened
4 ounces (½ cup) cream cheese, softened
¾ cup sugar
1 egg yolk
1½ teaspoons pure vanilla extract
¼ teaspoon salt
2¼ cups flour

CHOCOLATE GLAZE:

8 ounces semisweet chocolate, chopped coarse (or 1⅓ cups semisweet chocolate morsels)
2 tablespoons solid vegetable shortening

1. Preheat the oven to 350°F. Lightly butter two baking sheets; set aside.

2. Cream the butter, cream cheese, and sugar in an electric mixer at medium speed. Add the egg yolk, then the vanilla and salt, mixing until smooth. Lower the mixer speed and add the flour, mixing just until blended.

3. Divide the dough into quarters. Cut each portion into 10 equal walnut-size pieces. On a floured work surface, roll each piece into a smooth rope about 8 inches long. Bring the ends of each rope around in a pretzel shape. Lift the pretzels with a spatula and place them gently on the baking sheets, slightly apart.

4. Bake 10 minutes. With a spatula, gently transfer the pretzels to a wire rack to cool completely.

5. CHOCOLATE GLAZE: Melt the chocolate and the vegetable shortening in the top of a double boiler, stirring occasionally, until the chocolate is smooth and glossy. Transfer to a narrow bowl. (The chocolate should be deep enough to dip the cookies in halfway.) Set aside in a warm place, or in a shallow dish of warm water so the mixture remains fluid.

6. Place a wire rack over a sheet of wax paper. Dip the bottom of each cooled pretzel into the warm chocolate, coating it only halfway, and letting excess chocolate drip back into the bowl. Place the dipped cookies on the wire rack. Cool until set.

KITCHEN SINK GRANOLA BARS

Better than any granola bars you can buy, these are quick and easy to press into the pan, and loaded with dried fruit and nuts. (The crunchy, glazed coating might remind you of Cracker Jacks.)

Makes 27 bars, 3 × 1½ inches

Vegetable oil
2¼ cups granola
1 cup coarse-chopped salted dry-roasted peanuts
¾ cups raisins
⅓ cup chopped dates
⅓ cup chopped dried apricots
⅔ cup coconut, sweetened or unsweetened
¼ cup wheat germ
6 tablespoons (¾ stick) unsalted butter, cut in pieces
½ cup brown sugar
3 tablespoons light corn syrup
2 tablespoons honey
1 teaspoon pure vanilla extract

1. Preheat the oven to 350°F. Line a 9 × 13-inch baking pan with foil, pressing to coat the bottom and sides of the pan smoothly. Rub the foil with a light coating of vegetable oil; set aside.

2. In a large mixing bowl, stir together the granola, peanuts, raisins, dates, apricots, coconut, and wheat germ. Heat the butter, brown sugar, corn syrup, and honey in a saucepan over medium heat, stirring until the sugar has dissolved. Remove from heat and stir in the vanilla. Add this mixture to the mixing bowl, and stir with a wooden spoon until the ingredients are well combined. Press the mixture into the prepared baking pan, flattening the surface evenly with a palm dampened in cold water.

3. Bake 20 minutes. Place the baking pan on a wire rack to cool. When the mixture has cooled completely, invert the pan onto a cutting surface; then carefully peel off the foil. (Keep it bottom side up, so the shiny glazed bottom becomes the top.) Let the mixture stand at cool room temperature for an hour or two, to set the glaze. Pressing straight down with a large sharp knife, cut the mixture into three lengths 3 × 13 inches, and then cut each of these into 9 pieces 3 × 1½ inches. You should have twenty-seven 3 × 1½-inch bars. Store airtight. For lunchboxes or mailing, wrap the granola bars individually in plastic wrap, foil, or cellophane.

CHOCOLATE-DIPPED PEANUT BRITTLE FINGERS

A childhood favorite, reinterpreted as an irresistible cookie. These involve a few steps, but they're not difficult.

Makes 75 bars, 2 × 1 inch

BUTTER PASTRY DOUGH:

9 tablespoons (1 stick plus 1 tablespoon) unsalted butter, softened
½ cup plus 1 tablespoon sugar
1 egg
1 egg yolk
1 teaspoon pure vanilla extract
2¼ cups flour

PEANUT BRITTLE TOPPING:

6 tablespoons (¼ cup plus 2 tablespoons) light corn syrup
½ cup (packed) light brown sugar
¼ cup (½ stick) unsalted butter
¼ cup heavy cream
2 cups coarse-chopped peanuts, preferably salted dry-roasted (about 10 ounces)
1 teaspoon pure vanilla extract
Few drops of lemon juice

1. **BUTTER PASTRY DOUGH:** Cream the butter and sugar in an electric mixer at medium speed until light, about 3 minutes. Add the egg, egg yolk, and vanilla, beating until smooth. Add the flour, mixing just until blended, no longer. Pat the dough into the bottom of a 10½ × 15½-inch jelly roll pan (don't use a nonstick pan for this recipe), pressing it up the sides of the pan slightly. Refrigerate for about 15 minutes while you preheat the oven to 350°F.

2. Prick the surface of the dough with a fork. Bake on the center rack of the oven until the pastry is lightly golden, 15 to 18 minutes.

3. **PEANUT BRITTLE TOPPING:** Place the corn syrup, brown sugar, butter, and cream in a heavy saucepan and bring to a rolling boil, stirring to dissolve the sugar. Remove from heat and stir in the peanuts, vanilla, and lemon juice. Pour the topping over the pastry, spreading it gently with a spatula. (Take care not to tear the pastry.)

4. Return the pan to the oven and bake until the brittle topping is golden and bubbly, about 15 minutes. Place the pan on a wire rack and cool completely.

CHOCOLATE GLAZE:

6 ounces milk chocolate or semisweet chocolate, chopped coarse (or substitute 1 cup milk chocolate or semisweet chocolate morsels)

2 tablespoons solid vegetable shortening

5. **CHOCOLATE GLAZE:** Melt the chocolate and the vegetable shortening in the top of a double boiler, stirring occasionally, until the chocolate is smooth and glossy. Transfer to a narrow bowl. (The chocolate should be deep enough to dip the cookies in halfway.) Set aside in a warm place, or in a shallow dish of warm water, so the mixture remains fluid.

6. When the cookies have cooled completely, trim off the edges of the pastry, using a sharp knife and a ruler as a guide. Cut the pastry into 2 × 1-inch bars. Place a large wire rack over a sheet of wax paper. Dip the short end of each bar into the warm chocolate, coating it only halfway, and letting excess chocolate drip back into the bowl. Place the dipped cookies on the wire rack; cool until set.

GIANT STACKED COOKIE CAKE

Perfect for a kids' party—let them build their own cake. You can make this with Toll House cookies, too, or with your favorite recipe, or with Chunky White Chocolate–Macadamia Cookies (see page 64), forming giant cookies as directed below. And use any flavor of ice cream you like.

Serves 6 to 8

GIANT OATMEAL COOKIES:

- ½ cup (1 stick) butter, softened
- 1 cup (packed) brown sugar (either light or dark)
- 1 egg
- ½ cup whole wheat flour
- ½ cup unbleached all-purpose flour
- 1 teaspoon cinnamon
- 1 teaspoon baking powder
- ½ teaspoon baking soda
- ¼ teaspoon salt
- 1½ cups regular or quick-cooking oats (not instant oatmeal)
- ½ cup coarse-broken nuts (walnuts, pecans, etc.)

TOPPING:

- ⅔ cup semisweet chocolate morsels (or 4 ounces semisweet chocolate, chopped coarse)

1. **GIANT OATMEAL COOKIES:** Preheat the oven to 400°F. Butter two baking sheets; set aside.

2. Cream the butter and sugar in an electric mixer at medium speed until light, about 3 minutes. Add the egg and continue to beat until the mixture is smooth. Meanwhile, mix together the dry ingredients: whole wheat flour, unbleached flour, cinnamon, baking powder, baking soda, and salt. Add this mixture to the butter, mixing until blended. Stir in the oatmeal and nuts.

3. Spoon a scant ⅔ cup of the dough into a 1-cup dry measure, pressing it down evenly. Unmold the dough onto a baking sheet and spread it with a wet spoon into a neat 6-inch circle about ⅝ inch thick. Repeat with remaining dough, forming 5 uniform cookies.

4. Bake until the cookies begin to turn golden brown around the edges, about 11 minutes. (If you're baking both sheets at the same time, exchange the positions of the sheets halfway through baking so the cookies brown evenly.)

5. **TOPPING:** Remove one of the pans from the oven and quickly scatter the chocolate chips over one cookie (choose a nice round one—this will be the top of the cake), covering the entire surface. By this time the other cookie should be golden brown around the edges;

remove it to a rack. Return the pan to the oven and bake until the chips are softened, about 1 minute longer. Remove from the oven. Cool the cookies on the baking sheets; then use two spatulas to transfer them carefully to a wire rack.

FILLING:

1 quart vanilla ice cream (or your favorite flavor)

6. **FILLING:** Soften the ice cream slightly in the refrigerator. Clear enough space in your freezer for a large dinner plate. Place one cookie on a large, flat serving plate. Top with 1 cup of the ice cream, spreading it gently to cover the cookie, but leaving a narrow border around the edges. Place a second cookie on top, pressing gently. Repeat layering, topping the cake with the chocolate chip-covered cookie. Freeze the cake until firm. Cut into wedges with a large chef's knife.

Spumette

Chunky White Chocolate–Macadamia Cookies

Heavenly Hash Break-Up

Coconut-Chip Blondies

Giant Peanut Butter Top Hats

Disappearing Double Chocolate Brownies

Impossibly Rich Chocolate Pudding Cups

Milk Chocolate–Toasted Almond Candy Bar Cookies

More Cookies for Chocolate Lovers

What is it about chocolate that makes people go unashamedly *crazy* the moment it appears? Scientists have tried to explain this phenomenon—it seems there's a chemical substance in cocoa beans called phenylethylamine that, when released in your brain, causes the same chemical reaction as that which occurs when you're in love.

For the true chocolate lover, though, there's no explaining the pleasure of chocolate—or even describing it. As the chocolate—and only the best, please—melts down your throat, bells of pure pleasure just go off.

Chocolate lovers do not agree on the best way to enjoy chocolate in cookie form. Some flavor the cookie dough with melted chocolate or cocoa, for overall chocolate flavor. Others feel that this doesn't provide a "pure enough hit," and prefer that the chocolate be kept whole, in the form of chips or chunks, folded into a non-chocolate dough.

Here's a collection that includes both types.

DEALING WITH CHOCOLATE

Take extra care whenever you melt chocolate—if the chocolate is over-heated even slightly, it can burn or become grainy. For best results:

- Chop the chocolate in rough-cut pieces before melting.
- Melt the chocolate in a double boiler, over (not in) hot (not boiling) water, to insure smooth results.
- If you don't have a double boiler, you can melt chocolate in a small heavy pan over a Flame Tamer or asbestos pad. If necessary, you can work over very low direct heat, provided you stir the melting chocolate often.
- Remove the chocolate from the heat when there are still a few solid pieces left. Stir well; the heat from the melted chocolate will melt the remaining pieces, and the mixture will soon be perfectly smooth.

SPUMETTE

These chocolate-hazelnut meringues started out as a completely different cookie, and through gradual changes during testing, wound up being one of the best recipes in the book. They're light as can be, with a crisp, crackled top, and intensely chocolate, melt-in-your-mouth interiors. A nonstick pan is a big help for baking them.

Makes about 3 dozen 2½-inch cookies

1 ½ **cups hazelnuts, with skins (about 6 ounces)**
  1 **cup plus 2 tablespoons confectioners' sugar**
  3 **tablespoons best-quality unsweetened cocoa powder**
  ¼ **teaspoon cinnamon**
  3 **egg whites**
    Pinch of salt

1. Preheat the oven to 300°F. Butter and flour three baking sheets, preferably nonstick (or use sheets of aluminum foil); set aside. Place the hazelnuts in a cake pan and toast in the oven until fragrant, about 10 minutes. Rub the nuts between layers of kitchen towels to remove some of the skins (some bits of skin will remain; that's fine). Chop the hazelnuts very coarse; set aside.

2. Sift the confectioners' sugar with the cocoa powder and cinnamon onto a sheet of wax paper; set aside.

3. Beat the egg whites with the salt just until they form stiff peaks, but are still moist. With a large rubber spatula, very gently fold the confectioners' sugar mixture into the beaten egg whites, adding the mixture in three portions. Gently fold in the nuts. (The batter must now be used immediately, or it will deflate.)

4. Drop the batter onto the prepared baking sheets, using a level tablespoonful per cookie, and spacing them 2 inches apart.

5. Bake until dry to the touch (but still soft), with a shiny, crackled surface, 14 or 15 minutes—do not overbake. Very gently transfer the cookies with a spatula to a wire rack; cool completely.

CHUNKY WHITE CHOCOLATE–MACADAMIA COOKIES

These luxurious cookies, with the delicious combination of white chocolate and macadamia nuts, are showing up at expensive cookie shops around the country; here's how to make your own at home. It's likely that Debbie (Mrs.) Fields started this craze—but did you know that macadamia nuts were named for John Macadam, a 19th-century Australian chemist?

Makes about 30 cookies, 2 inches in diameter

½ cup (1 stick) unsalted butter, softened
½ cup light brown sugar
¼ cup granulated sugar
1 egg
1 teaspoon pure vanilla extract
1 cup plus 2 teaspoons flour
½ teaspoon baking soda
¼ teaspoon salt
5 thick bars (1.8 ounces each) white chocolate with almonds, or three 3-ounce bars imported white chocolate, cut into ⅜-inch chunks (about 1¾ cups)
1 cup coarse-chopped unsalted macadamia nuts

1. Preheat the oven to 375°F. Lightly butter two cookie sheets; set aside.

2. In an electric mixer, cream the butter with the brown and granulated sugars at medium speed until light, about 3 minutes. Add the egg, then the vanilla, mixing until blended.

3. Meanwhile, sift the flour with the baking soda and salt onto a sheet of wax paper. Lower the mixer speed and add the flour, mixing just until blended, no longer. Add the white chocolate chunks and macadamia nuts and stir just until evenly distributed.

4. Roll rounded tablespoonfuls of the dough between your palms to make neat balls. Place on the baking sheets and gently flatten. Bake the cookies until lightly golden, 9 to 12 minutes. Transfer to a wire rack and cool completely.

HEAVENLY HASH BREAK-UP

The old favorite chocolate-marshmallow-nut candy, baked in a huge, crisp cookie sheet, from which everyone breaks off his or her own pieces. Or try breaking the baked cookie sheet into smaller pieces, and folding them into vanilla or coffee ice cream. Mmmmm. . . .

Makes one 15½ × 10½-inch sheet

1 **cup flour**
2 **tablespoons unsweetened cocoa powder**
½ **teaspoon baking soda**
¼ **teaspoon salt**
½ **cup (1 stick) unsalted butter, softened**
¾ **cup sugar**
1 **egg**
½ **teaspoon pure vanilla extract**
1 **cup semisweet chocolate morsels (6 ounces)**
1¼ **cups coarse-broken walnuts or pecans**
1 **cup miniature marshmallows (or 8 to 10 quartered large marshmallows)**

1. Preheat the oven to 350°F. Line a 15½ × 10½-inch jelly roll pan with aluminum foil, pressing to coat the bottom and sides of the pan smoothly. Butter the foil; set aside.

2. Sift the flour, cocoa, baking soda, and salt onto a sheet of wax paper; set aside. In an electric mixer, cream the butter and sugar at medium speed until light. Add the egg and vanilla, beating until well blended. Lower the mixer speed and mix in the flour mixture just until blended, no longer. Stir in the chocolate morsels and walnuts.

3. With palms moistened in cold water, pat the dough into the bottom of the pan, so that it covers the pan evenly. You won't be able to cover it completely; don't worry about some holes in the batter.

4. Bake 18 minutes, or until lightly puffed and the surface is dry (but still soft). Scatter the marshmallows over the surface, very gently pressing them into the chocolate mixture (careful—it's still very hot!). Bake 2 minutes longer. Remove the pan from the oven and cool on a wire rack.

5. When the mixture has cooled completely, invert the pan onto a baking sheet and carefully peel off the foil. Let everyone break off his or her own pieces of the hash.

COCONUT-CHIP BLONDIES

The combination of chocolate and coconut, which has made many Mounds bar fans, has here been transformed into a moist bar cookie, generously studded with semisweet chocolate chips, coconut, and pecans.

Makes about 2 dozen 3 × 1-inch bars

½ cup (1 stick) unsalted butter, softened
⅓ cup granulated sugar
⅓ cup brown sugar
1 egg
1 teaspoon pure vanilla extract
1 cup plus 2 tablespoons flour
½ teaspoon baking soda
¼ teaspoon salt
1 cup semisweet chocolate morsels (a 6-ounce package)
1 ¼ cups shredded coconut, sweetened or unsweetened
½ cup chopped pecans

1. Preheat the oven to 350°F. Butter a 9-inch square baking pan; set aside. In an electric mixer, cream the butter with the granulated and brown sugars at medium speed until light. Add the egg, then the vanilla, mixing until blended.

2. Meanwhile, sift the flour with the baking soda and salt onto a sheet of wax paper. Lower the mixer speed and add the flour, mixing just until blended, no longer. Add the chocolate morsels, coconut, and pecans and mix just until evenly distributed. Transfer the dough to the baking pan, spreading it evenly.

3. Bake 20 minutes, or until the top is dry and golden brown, and a toothpick inserted in the center of the mixture comes out nearly clean. Cool the pan on a wire rack, then cut into 27 bars.

GIANT PEANUT BUTTER TOP HATS

A moist, chewy cookie topped with a thick layer of chocolate. You can also try these as "chunk-ins"—breaking up the cookies and folding them into vanilla ice cream.

Makes 2 dozen 4-inch cookies

½ cup (1 stick) unsalted butter, softened
¾ cup chunky peanut butter
½ cup granulated sugar
½ cup light brown sugar
1 egg
2 tablespoons molasses
1 teaspoon pure vanilla extract
1¾ cups flour
1 teaspoon baking soda

TOPPING:

6 bars (1.45 ounces each) milk chocolate, each cut into 4 large squares, or 1⅓ cups milk chocolate morsels

1. Preheat the oven to 375°F. Butter four baking sheets (or sheets of aluminum foil); set aside. In an electric mixer at medium speed, beat the butter and peanut butter until well combined. Gradually add the granulated and brown sugars, beating until fluffy. Add the egg, molasses, and vanilla, beating until well blended.

2. Meanwhile, sift the flour and baking soda onto a sheet of wax paper. Lower the mixer speed and add the flour mixture, mixing just until blended; do not overbeat.

3. Using two spoons, drop the dough onto the baking sheets in neat rows, using a heaping tablespoon of dough for each cookie, and spacing them well apart —these cookies will spread. Bake 7 minutes, or until the cookies are set and just very lightly browned (don't overbake at this stage—they will be baked longer).

4. TOPPING: Working quickly, place a square of chocolate or about ½ ounce chocolate morsels on each cookie. Return to the oven and bake until the cookies are browned and the chocolate has softened but still holds its shape, 1 or 2 minutes longer. Place the baking sheets on a wire rack and cool the cookies for about 5 minutes; then use a spatula to carefully transfer the cookies to the rack to cool. Serve lukewarm or at room temperature. A tall glass of cold milk is a must with these.

DISAPPEARING DOUBLE CHOCOLATE BROWNIES

Dedicated brownie lovers insist that fudgy brownies are the only true kind. And they don't come much fudgier than these. . . .

Makes 32 brownies, 1 × 2 inches (these are rich!)

1¼ **cups coarse-chopped pecans (about 4½ ounces)**

2 **ounces unsweetened chocolate, chopped coarse**

½ **cup (1 stick) unsalted butter, cut in pieces**

2 **eggs**

1 **cup sugar**

1 **teaspoon pure vanilla extract**

⅔ **cup flour**

½ **teaspoon baking powder**
Pinch of salt

4 **ounces semisweet chocolate, cut in coarse chunks (or substitute ⅔ cup semisweet chocolate morsels)**

1. Preheat the oven to 350°F. Lightly butter an 8-inch square baking pan; set aside. Toast the chopped pecans on a baking sheet until fragrant and lightly colored, about 7 minutes. Set aside to cool slightly.

2. Place the unsweetened chocolate and butter in a heavy saucepan and melt over low heat, stirring occasionally. Set aside to cool slightly.

3. In an electric mixer with the whisk attachment, whisk the eggs at medium speed until light and frothy, about 3 minutes. Gradually add the sugar, beating constantly. When all the sugar has been added, add the vanilla; then remove the bowl from the machine.

4. Meanwhile, sift the flour, baking powder, and salt onto a sheet of wax paper; set aside. When the egg-sugar mixture is ready, gently fold in the melted chocolate mixture with a large rubber spatula—don't incorporate it completely; there should still be a few streaks of chocolate visible. Now gently fold in the flour mixture. When that's not quite incorporated (just a couple of streaks of flour still showing), fold in the toasted pecans and the chocolate just until everything is well blended, no longer. Transfer the batter to the prepared pan, smoothing it gently to the edges of the pan.

5. Bake 25 minutes—the top should be dry, but a toothpick inserted in the center will emerge with some traces of melted chocolate. Place the pan on a rack and cool completely. Don't try to cut brownies when warm. When cool, cut into 32 bars.

IMPOSSIBLY RICH CHOCOLATE PUDDING CUPS

Miniature pies, with a silky filling that's richer than any chocolate pudding around. Try these as an after-dinner treat, instead of chocolate truffles.

Makes 2 dozen

⅓ recipe Carlo's Cookie Dough (see page 33), *or* use ½ recipe Lemon-Cream Cheese Dough (see page 50, but omit lemon zest), *or* about 10 ounces of your favorite pie pastry dough

IMPOSSIBLY RICH CHOCOLATE PUDDING:

4 ounces best-quality semisweet chocolate, chopped coarse (or substitute ⅔ cup semisweet chocolate morsels)
½ cup (1 stick) unsalted butter, softened
2 eggs, well beaten

1. Roll the pastry dough on a lightly floured surface to a thickness of ¹⁄₁₆ inch. With a 3-inch fluted round cutter, cut out rounds of dough and fit them into ungreased miniature (1¾-inch) muffin tins. Re-roll scraps of dough as necessary. Chill the pastry until firm, at least 30 minutes.

2. IMPOSSIBLY RICH CHOCOLATE PUDDING: Melt the chocolate over hot water; set aside to cool slightly. In an electric mixer, beat the butter at medium speed until smooth and light. Very gradually add the beaten eggs, beating constantly until smooth. Gradually add the chocolate, beating until very smooth and shiny. Cool the mixture to room temperature. (Do not refrigerate at this point.)

3. BAKING THE COOKIE SHELLS: Preheat the oven to 350°F. Prick the pastry gently with a fork. Bake until the pastry is lightly golden and baked through, pricking any air bubbles with a fork, 12 to 15 minutes. Cool the cookie shells completely, in their muffin tins, on a wire rack.

4. ASSEMBLY: When cool, carefully remove the pastry shells from the muffin tins. Spoon about 2 teaspoons of the chocolate pudding into each shell. If you're not serving the pudding cups right away, chill; then remove from the refrigerator about 30 minutes before serving to soften the filling. If you'd like to gild the lily, spoon a dab of vanilla-flavored whipped cream on each cup.

MILK CHOCOLATE–TOASTED ALMOND CANDY BAR COOKIES

Look out—these are intense! Like a cookie version of an almond milk chocolate bar, with as much chocolate as possible worked into the dough, and chunks, too. The milk chocolate gives these an entirely different flavor from the semisweet morsels usually used in chocolate chip cookies. Nonstick baking sheets work well with these. And don't overbake, or they won't have that candy-bar richness.

Makes 3 dozen 3-inch cookies

1 cup whole almonds, with skins

9 ounces milk chocolate, cut in ⅜-inch chunks (about 1½ cups)

2 ounces unsweetened chocolate, chopped coarse

¼ cup (½ stick) unsalted butter, cut in pieces

¼ cup flour

¼ teaspoon baking powder

¼ teaspoon salt

2 eggs

⅔ cup sugar

1 teaspoon instant coffee powder, preferably espresso, Nescafé Brava, or other full-flavored coffee

1 teaspoon pure vanilla extract

1. Preheat the oven to 350°F. Butter and flour three baking sheets or sheets of aluminum foil (or use nonstick sheets); set aside. Place the almonds on a baking pan; toast until fragrant, about 8 minutes. Chop the nuts coarse; set aside.

2. In a heavy saucepan, combine ¾ cup of the milk chocolate chunks with the unsweetened chocolate and the butter. Melt the mixture over low heat, stirring occasionally. Meanwhile, sift the flour, baking powder, and salt onto a sheet of wax paper; set aside.

3. In an electric mixer, beat the eggs, sugar, coffee, and vanilla at medium speed until the mixture forms a thick ribbon when dropped from the whisk or beaters, about 5 minutes.

4. Remove the mixture from the machine; gently fold in the chocolate mixture until not quite combined. Fold in the flour mixture just until combined; then add the remaining milk chocolate chunks and the chopped toasted almonds, folding gently just until incorporated. (This dough must be baked right away.)

5. Drop the dough by rounded tablespoonfuls onto the baking sheets, spacing them 1½ inches apart. Bake until the tops are set (but still quite soft), with a shiny, slightly crackled surface, 7 to 9 minutes. (If using lightweight baking sheets, they'll probably take only 7 minutes.) Do not overbake.

6. Remove the baking sheets from the oven and place them on a wire rack. Cool the cookies on the baking sheets. When they have cooled completely, transfer the cookies with a spatula to a plate or tin and store airtight.

More Cookies for Chocolate Lovers:

COOKIE HOT LINES

Having problems baking cookies? Help is just a toll-free call away. According to *Good Food* magazine, three major food companies offer hot lines to answer cookie emergencies—preferably involving their products. Call Monday through Friday:

- Pillsbury, 1-800-328-4466 (9:15 A.M.–8:45 P.M., Eastern time)
- General Mills, 1-800-328-6787 (8:30 A.M.–6:00 P.M., Eastern time)
- Duncan Hines, 1-800-543-7276 (9:30 A.M.–7:30 P.M., Eastern time)

SANDWICHES AND MORE

Mary's Fruit Rolls
Cream-Filled Cocoa Sandwiches
Chocolate Mousse Sandwiches
Jam Crunch
Whole-Grain Lemon Cream Sandwiches
Cream Cheese & Jelly Turnovers

Sandwich cookies are a breed unto themselves. Were you raised on Oreos and Hydrox? Children of the 50s remember having them as a late-night snack when "sleeping over," or being given a couple to soothe the pain of a skinned knee.

The purists—kids—say that in order to enjoy sandwich cookies at their best, you must first master the special technique of eating them:

1. Carefully separate the cookies, trying to keep the filling on one side only.

2. Discard the empty cookie.

3. Now eat the filling, scraping it off the cookie with your top front teeth.

Have you ever tried baking sandwich cookies at home? It's easy, and fun to put them together. Also, you can mix and match flavors, and the cookies will be fresher, too. In order to keep them crisp, you might want to fill only a small batch at a time.

MARY'S FRUIT ROLLS

From my friend Mary Codola in Rhode Island, these are almost like a home version of Fig Newtons—but more interesting, with several kinds of dried fruits and nuts in the moist filling. And the rum makes these a cookie that adults will like, too. (Don't worry about kids becoming tipsy—the alcohol bakes off, leaving just the rum flavor.)

Makes 4 dozen 1-inch slices

DOUGH:

- 4 **tablespoons (½ stick) unsalted butter, softened**
- 2 **ounces (¼ cup) cream cheese, softened**
- 2 **eggs**
- 1 **teaspoon pure vanilla extract**
- 1 **cup sugar**
- 2 **cups flour**
- 1½ **teaspoons baking powder**

1. **DOUGH**: Place the butter, cream cheese, eggs, vanilla, sugar, flour, and baking powder in the bowl of an electric mixer. Mix slowly until blended and smooth; do not overbeat. Gather the dough into a ball; place on a sheet of plastic wrap and sprinkle with flour. Wrap tight and chill until firm enough to be rolled out, at least 1 hour.

DRIED FRUIT FILLING:

1 **box (12 ounces) pitted prunes**
1 **cup dried figs (about 6 ounces)**
⅓ **cup golden raisins**
½ **cup coarse-chopped nuts**
  (walnuts, pecans, or almonds,
  or a combination)
3 **tablespoons honey**
3 **tablespoons dark rum or**
  Scotch (or substitute orange
  juice or apple cider)
1 **teaspoon cinnamon**
  Confectioners' sugar

2. **DRIED FRUIT FILLING:** Place the prunes, figs, raisins, and nuts in a food processor and pulse on and off until evenly chopped. (You can also chop the mixture with a large chef's knife; oil the blade to prevent sticking.) Transfer the mixture to a bowl and stir in the honey, rum, and cinnamon. Set aside.

3. Preheat the oven to 400°F. Lightly butter two baking sheets; set aside.

4. Divide the dough in quarters. Leaving the remainder refrigerated, roll out each portion of dough on a lightly floured surface to a rectangle about 12 × 5 inches. Spread about ¾ cup of the fruit filling down the center of the dough. Wrap one long side of dough up over the filling; then bring up the other side, overlapping slightly and pressing the seam gently to seal. With a long spatula, transfer the filled roll to a baking sheet, seam down. Chill the roll while filling remainder of dough; place two rolls on each baking sheet, spacing them well apart.

5. Bake until lightly golden, 15 to 17 minutes. Place the baking sheets on a wire rack to cool; then sprinkle the rolls with confectioners' sugar and cut diagonally in 1-inch slices. (The ends are reserved for you.) Store the cookies airtight. These cookies freeze well, unsliced and tightly wrapped.

CREAM-FILLED COCOA SANDWICHES

"Black" cookies with a white filling (below), "white" ones filled with black (next recipe). Take your pick—or make both, for an Art Deco look.

Makes about 32 sandwiches

COCOA COOKIES:

- ¾ **cup (1½ sticks) unsalted butter, softened**
- ¾ **cup sugar**
- 2 **eggs**
- 1½ **teaspoons pure vanilla extract**
- 1½ **cups flour**
- ½ **cup unsweetened cocoa powder**
- ¼ **teaspoon baking powder**
- ¼ **teaspoon baking soda**
- ⅛ **teaspoon salt**
- ½ **cup chopped walnuts**

VANILLA OR COFFEE CREAM FILLING:

- ½ **cup (1 stick) unsalted butter, softened**
- 1⅓ **cups confectioners' sugar**
- 2 **teaspoons pure vanilla extract**
- 2 **teaspoons instant coffee, preferably instant espresso, Nescafé Brava, or other full-flavored coffee (optional)**
- 1 **teaspoon hot water (optional)**

1. **COCOA COOKIES:** Cream the butter and sugar in an electric mixer at medium speed. Add the eggs, one at a time, then the vanilla. Meanwhile, sift together the flour, cocoa powder, baking powder, baking soda, and salt onto a sheet of wax paper. Lower the mixer speed and add the flour mixture, then the walnuts, mixing just until blended, no longer. Wrap the dough in plastic wrap and chill until firm enough to be rolled out, at least 2 hours.

2. Preheat the oven to 350°F. Lightly butter three baking sheets (or sheets of aluminum foil); set aside.

3. Divide the dough in thirds. Place one portion of dough on a well-floured surface, keeping the remainder refrigerated. Roll out the dough to a thickness of ⅛ inch. Brush off excess flour with a soft, dry pastry brush. Cut out 2-inch rounds of dough with a fluted or plain cookie cutter dipped in flour. Using a floured spatula, transfer the cookies to the baking sheets, spacing them about ½ inch apart. (This dough is quite soft, and must be handled carefully; return the dough to the refrigerator if it becomes difficult to work with.) Repeat with remaining dough, and reroll chilled scraps.

4. Bake the cookies until set and the centers are dry to the touch, 10 to 12 minutes (do not overbake). Transfer to a wire rack to cool completely. The cookies will become crisper as they cool.

5. **VANILLA OR COFFEE CREAM FILLING:** In an electric mixer or food processor, blend the butter and confectioners' sugar until smooth; blend in the vanilla. To flavor the filling with coffee, stir together the instant coffee and hot water in a small cup; then stir this into the vanilla filling. (If you like, fill half the cookies with vanilla filling, and half with coffee filling.) Chill the filling, stirring every few minutes, until slightly firm but still spreadable, about 20 minutes.

6. **ASSEMBLY:** With a small spatula, top half the cooled cookies with the cream filling, spreading about 2 teaspoons of filling on the flat bottom of each cookie. Top each filled cookie with a plain cookie, pressing the flat bottom lightly onto the filling. Store and serve at cool room temperature. (In warm weather, these cookies should be refrigerated.)

CHOCOLATE MOUSSE SANDWICHES

To keep these cookies crisp, they should be assembled shortly before they are served.

Makes 30 sandwiches

BUTTER COOKIES DELUXE:

1 cup (2 sticks) unsalted butter, softened
1 cup sugar
1 teaspoon pure vanilla extract
2 eggs
2 cups flour

WHIPPED GANACHE FUDGE FILLING:

1½ cups heavy cream
6 ounces best-quality semisweet chocolate, chopped coarse (or substitute 1 cup semisweet chocolate morsels)

1. **BUTTER COOKIES DELUXE:** In an electric mixer, cream the butter and sugar at medium speed until very light, 3 to 5 minutes. Add the vanilla, then the eggs, one at a time. Lower the speed and add the flour, mixing just until well blended, no longer. Chill overnight, or at least 4 hours.

2. Preheat the oven to 350°F. Lightly butter four baking sheets (or sheets of foil). Divide the dough in quarters. Place one portion of dough on a lightly floured surface, keeping the remainder refrigerated. Roll out the dough to a thickness of ¼ inch. Cut out 2-inch circles with a fluted or plain cookie cutter dipped in flour. (Alternatively, you can cut the dough into rectangles, using a fluted pastry wheel.) Place the cookies on the baking sheets, spacing them about 1 inch apart. Repeat with remaining dough, and reroll chilled scraps.

3. Bake the cookies until the edges are light golden brown, 7 to 8 minutes. Transfer to a wire rack to cool completely.

4. **WHIPPED GANACHE FUDGE FILLING:** Bring the cream to a boil in a heavy saucepan. Add the chocolate and remove the pan from the heat. Let the mixture stand briefly; then stir until smooth. Transfer to a metal bowl and chill thoroughly, stirring once in a while. (If you'd like to hasten the process, place the metal bowl in a larger bowl of ice water; stir the chocolate mixture until cool.) With a whisk or an electric mixer, whip the chocolate mixture just until fluffy, about 1 minute; do not overwhip, or it will separate.

5. **ASSEMBLY**: Spread half the cooled cookies (on their flat, bottom side) with the chocolate filling, using a small spatula and about 1 tablespoon of filling for each cookie. Top each filled cookie with a plain cookie, pressing flat bottom lightly onto the filling. Chill briefly to set the filling slightly; then serve at cool room temperature. In warm weather, these cookies should be refrigerated; remove from the refrigerator a few minutes before serving.

JAM CRUNCH

A layered sandwich of crunchy oat shortbread, with liqueur-spiked jam peeking through in between.

Makes 64 squares

½ cup (1 stick) plus 2 tablespoons cold unsalted butter, cut in pieces
1¼ cups flour
1¼ cups regular or quick-cooking oats (not instant oatmeal)
1 cup (packed) light brown sugar
Pinch of salt
¾ cup (generous) black currant, raspberry, or other dark jam
2 tablespoons crème de cassis, raspberry liqueur, or brandy
½ cup chopped almonds

1. Preheat the oven to 375°F. Generously butter an 8-inch square baking pan; set aside.

2. In a food processor, combine the butter, flour, oatmeal, brown sugar, and salt until crumbly (if you don't have a processor, cut the ingredients together with two butter knives). Press about two thirds of this mixture into the bottom of the pan.

3. In a small bowl, stir together the jam and the liqueur. Use a spoon to spread the jam mixture very gently over the bottom oatmeal layer. Stir the almonds into the remaining third of the oatmeal mixture; scatter this evenly over the jam. Very gently press the top layer smooth.

4. Bake until set and golden brown, 40 to 45 minutes. Cool the pan on a wire rack. When completely cool, carefully cut the mixture into 1-inch squares. Store airtight.

WHOLE-GRAIN LEMON CREAM SANDWICHES

An English favorite.

Makes 2 dozen sandwiches

Double recipe Whole-Grain Wafers (p. 107)

LEMON CREAM FILLING:

½ **cup (1 stick) unsalted butter, softened**
1⅓ **cups confectioners' sugar**
   Grated zest of 1 lemon
2 **teaspoons fresh lemon juice**

1. Bake the Whole-Grain Wafers as directed; cool completely.

2. **LEMON CREAM FILLING:** In an electric mixer or food processor, blend the butter and sugar until smooth. Add the lemon zest and juice, mixing until smooth. Chill the filling, stirring every few minutes, until slightly firm but still spreadable, about 20 minutes.

3. **ASSEMBLY:** Top half the cooled cookies with the filling, using a small spatula to spread about 2 teaspoons of filling on the flat bottom of each cookie. Top each filled cookie with a plain cookie, pressing the flat bottom lightly onto the filling. Refrigerate briefly to firm up the filling; then store and serve at cool room temperature. (In warm weather, these cookies should be refrigerated.)

CREAM CHEESE & JELLY TURNOVERS

Tiny turnovers; try baking these with two or three different kinds of preserves, making a few with each kind.

Makes 4 dozen turnovers

1 **recipe Lemon–Cream Cheese Dough (page 50), or substitute 1¼ pounds of your favorite pie pastry dough**
1 **jar (12 ounces) thick cherry preserves**
   Confectioners' sugar

1. Preheat the oven to 375°F. Roll half the dough on a lightly floured surface to a thickness of ⅛ inch (keep the remainder refrigerated). With a fluted round cutter, cut out 2½-inch rounds of dough. If, at any point, the dough becomes too soft to handle easily, refrigerate until firm. Roll the remaining dough, and reroll scraps.

2. ASSEMBLY: Moisten the rims of the rounds of dough with a finger dipped in cold water. Dab about ¼ teaspoon of jam on each round of dough, placing it slightly off center. Fold the dough over the jam, pressing the edges to seal. Transfer the turnovers to two lightly greased baking sheets.

3. Bake until lightly golden, about 15 minutes. Transfer to a baking sheet to cool. Serve at room temperature or slightly warm, sprinkled with confectioners' sugar.

MINIATURES

The World's Best Rogelach
Baby Fruitcakes
New York Cheesecake Squares
Virginia Hazelnut Bars
Little Butterscotch Pies
Caramelized Almond Spirals
Other Miniatures

I can't explain why, but there's something especially satisfying about being served a little individual cake or pie, all your own. Sure, a piece of pie, cake, or fruitcake can be delicious (well, with fruitcake, sometimes). But when you have a perfect little neat-edged square of pecan pie or cheesecake, or a tiny croissant-shaped rogelach, the taste seems even better. And because you can easily convince yourself you're not eating as much, you can go back for seconds. And thirds.

THE WORLD'S BEST ROGELACH

You can easily find recipes for these Jewish, filled crescent cookies—but not for ones this good. Ruth Cousineau really knows what she's doing. Her trick: "Don't overmix this dough—as soon as it comes together, that's it!" The result: a tender, buttery pastry, with a beautifully flaky texture.

Rogelach never taste as good as when they're freshly baked. If you'd like to freeze them, freeze them shaped, but unbaked (through Step 4). Then place them, still frozen, on a baking sheet, defrost briefly in the refrigerator, and bake as instructed.

Makes about 4 dozen

SOUR CREAM PASTRY DOUGH:

- **2 cups flour**
- **1 cup (2 sticks) cold unsalted butter, cut in small pieces**
- **1 egg yolk**
- **¾ cup sour cream**

Choose one of these fillings:

CHOCOLATE-WALNUT FILLING:

- **2 ounces semisweet chocolate (or substitute ⅓ cup semisweet chocolate morsels)**
- **½ ounce unsweetened chocolate**
- **⅓ cup walnut pieces**
- **3 tablespoons sugar**
- **½ teaspoon cinnamon**

1. SOUR CREAM PASTRY DOUGH: Place the flour, butter, egg yolk, and sour cream in the bowl of an electric mixer. Mix at low speed just until the dough comes together, no longer. Wrap the dough in plastic wrap and chill until firm, overnight if possible.

2. FILLING: Place the ingredients for whichever filling you choose in a food processor and pulse until finely chopped. Transfer to a mixing bowl; set aside.

3. ASSEMBLY: Preheat the oven to 350°F. Divide the dough in four equal pieces. Roll one piece of dough on a lightly floured surface to a 9-inch circle, leaving the remaining pieces refrigerated. Spread one quarter of the filling over the surface of the dough (you'll need about 2½ tablespoons of the chocolate-walnut filling; ¼ cup of the prune or dried fruit fillings). If you are using the chocolate-walnut filling, press it gently into the dough.

4. With a sharp knife, cut the circle in 12 neat wedges (a pizza cutter works great for this). Beginning with the outside edge, roll the wedges up tight toward

PRUNE FILLING:

1 cup (6 ounces) pitted prunes
3 tablespoons honey
2 tablespoons orange juice
½ teaspoon grated orange zest

DRIED FRUIT FILLING:

⅓ recipe Dried Fruit Filling
(p. 77)

TOPPING:

2 tablespoons unsalted butter,
melted
3 tablespoons sugar
½ teaspoon cinnamon

the center and place them on an ungreased baking sheet, tucking the center points underneath and spacing them about ½ inch apart. Repeat with remaining dough and filling. Keep the assembled rogelach refrigerated while you work on the remainder.

5. **TOPPING:** Brush the rogelach very lightly with melted butter. Combine the sugar and cinnamon; sprinkle the rogelach with a light coating of the cinnamon sugar.

6. Bake the rogelach until golden brown, about 30 minutes. Transfer them immediately to a wire rack to cool. Serve lukewarm or at room temperature, with tea, coffee, or a glass of cold milk.

Rogelach Variations:

- You can also make rogelach with Incredibly Quick Puff Pastry (page 96), for a flakier, more croissant-like texture.
- For hors d'oeuvre "mini-croissants," prepare rogelach as directed above, using either the dough above, or Incredibly Quick Puff Pastry (page 96). In Step 3, roll out as directed, spread with a little Dijon mustard, then sprinkle with grated Swiss or Parmesan cheese, then with slivers of ham around the outer edge. Roll up, bake as directed, and serve hot.

BABY FRUITCAKES

There are so many less-than-wonderful fruitcakes around that plenty of people say they'll be happy if they never see a fruitcake again. These are something else entirely—tiny glazed cakes, chunky with the best dried fruits and nuts (rather than commercial chopped candied fruit), bound with a minimum of spice cake batter. You'll need miniature muffin tins for these, though a regular-size muffin pan can also be used. Nonstick pans are a big help here, as are paper muffin liners.

Makes 2 dozen 1½-inch miniature cupcakes, or 1 dozen muffin-size

½ cup *each* raisins, golden raisins, dried currants, and chopped dates
⅓ cup chopped dried pineapple
⅓ cup chopped candied cherries
3 tablespoons chopped crystallized ginger
3 tablespoons bourbon or brandy (or apple cider)
¼ cup (½ stick) unsalted butter, softened
⅓ cup light brown sugar
1 egg
½ cup flour
¾ teaspoon ground allspice
½ teaspoon cinnamon
½ teaspoon fresh-grated nutmeg
¼ teaspoon ground cloves
¼ teaspoon salt
⅛ teaspoon baking powder
⅛ teaspoon baking soda
⅓ cup *each* coarsely chopped walnuts, pecans, and almonds

1. Place the raisins, golden raisins, currants, dates, pineapple, cherries, and crystallized ginger in a bowl. Toss with the bourbon and set aside to soak at least 30 minutes.

2. Preheat the oven to 300°F., with racks in the center and bottom of the oven. Place a pan of hot water on the lower rack. Line miniature or regular-size muffin tins with paper muffin liners. If you don't have paper liners, butter the pan(s) generously.

3. Cream the butter and brown sugar in an electric mixer until light; then add the egg, mixing until smooth. Meanwhile, sift together the flour, allspice, cinnamon, nutmeg, cloves, salt, baking powder, and baking soda onto a sheet of wax paper. Lower the mixer speed and add the flour mixture to the creamed mixture, mixing just until blended, no longer. Stir in the fruit mixture with its soaking liquid, along with the walnuts, pecans, and almonds, mixing just until incorporated.

4. Bake the fruitcakes until lightly golden and a toothpick inserted in the center emerges clean, about 30 minutes (or 35 for regular-size muffin tins). Cool in the pan(s) for about 5 minutes; then run the tip of a

BOURBON GLAZE:

2 **tablespoons light corn syrup**
2 **teaspoons bourbon or brandy**
   (or apple cider)

knife blade around the cakes and remove from the pan(s) (leave the paper liners on), placing them on a wire rack over a sheet of wax paper.

    5. **BOURBON GLAZE:** Place the corn syrup in a small pan and heat gently, just to thin it. Remove from heat, stir in the bourbon, and brush the tops of the fruitcakes with the glaze. Let stand until set; then store airtight. These keep well for at least a week, and can be mailed.

NEW YORK CHEESECAKE SQUARES

Firm enough to cut into neat squares, creamy enough to satisfy the most demanding cheesecake fans.

Makes 64 squares

GINGER CRUMB CRUST:

7 **ounces gingersnaps or ginger wafers, broken into pieces**
¼ **cup (½ stick) unsalted butter, softened**

CHEESECAKE FILLING:

1 **pound cream cheese (about 2 cups), softened**
¾ **cup sugar**
  Grated zest of ½ lemon
2 **eggs**
2 **tablespoons sour cream**
1 **tablespoon lemon juice**
1½ **teaspoons pure vanilla extract**

GLAZE:

½ **cup good orange marmalade**

1. **GINGER CRUMB CRUST:** Preheat the oven to 300°F. Butter an 8-inch square pan. Finely grind the cookies in a food processor (you should have about 1¾ cups); add the soft butter and process until blended. Press the crumb mixture into the bottom of the baking pan and bake 6 minutes. Cool briefly while you make the filling.

2. **CHEESECAKE FILLING:** Beat the cream cheese in an electric mixer until very smooth. Add the sugar and lemon zest and continue to beat until well blended. Add the eggs, one at a time; then the sour cream, lemon juice, and vanilla, mixing until very smooth. Transfer the mixture to the baking pan, spreading it smooth with a spatula over the crumb crust.

3. Bake until set and the surface is gently but uniformly puffed, about 40 minutes. Cool the pan completely on a wire rack, then refrigerate until firm.

4. **GLAZE:** Warm the marmalade until spreadable. Working gently, brush an even layer of marmalade over the chilled surface of the cheesecake. Chill again. Cut the cheesecake into 1-inch squares with a long thin knife dipped frequently in hot water. This cake will keep for a day or two, refrigerated. (If not serving all the squares at one time, cut only as many pieces as you need, placing a sheet of plastic wrap against the cut edges.)

VIRGINIA HAZELNUT BARS

Like miniature pecan pies, but with the distinctive flavor of toasted hazelnuts.

Makes 32 bars, or 64 squares

BUTTER DOUGH:

- **6 tablespoons (¾ stick) unsalted butter, softened**
- **¼ cup plus 2 tablespoons sugar**
- **¾ teaspoon grated lemon zest (from half a large lemon)**
- **1 egg**
- **½ teaspoon pure vanilla extract**
- **1½ cups flour**

HAZELNUT TOPPING:

- **1½ cups whole hazelnuts, with skins**
- **½ cup (1 stick) unsalted butter, cut up**
- **½ cup light brown sugar**
- **½ cup honey**
- **2 tablespoons heavy cream**
- **1 teaspoon pure vanilla extract**
- **¼ teaspoon fresh lemon juice**

1. **BUTTER DOUGH:** Preheat the oven to 350°F. Butter and flour an 8-inch square baking pan. In an electric mixer, cream the butter, sugar, and lemon zest at medium speed until light, about 3 minutes. Add the egg and vanilla and beat until smooth. Lower the mixer speed slightly and add the flour, mixing just until well combined. Press the dough into the bottom of the pan to an even thickness of ¼ inch. Prick the dough with a fork; then bake until pale gold, about 12 minutes.

2. **HAZELNUT TOPPING:** Place the hazelnuts in a cake pan and toast in the oven until fragrant, about 10 minutes. Rub the nuts between layers of a kitchen towel to remove some of the skins (some bits of skin will remain; that's fine). Chop the nuts coarse; set aside.

3. In a heavy saucepan, bring the butter, brown sugar, and honey to a vigorous boil, stirring. Add the cream and boil the mixture for a few seconds. Remove from heat and stir in the vanilla, lemon juice, and the reserved hazelnuts. Pour over the partly baked dough.

4. Bake until the topping mixture is bubbling and almost set, about 30 minutes. Cool the pan on a wire rack. When completely cooled, run a thin knife blade around the edges of the pan; then carefully invert the pastry onto a wire rack. Lift off the pan; invert the pastry again onto a baking sheet. Gently slide the pastry from the baking sheet to a cutting surface. Trim edges if necessary. With a large heavy knife, cut the pastry into 1 × 2-inch bars or 1-inch squares. Store airtight.

LITTLE BUTTERSCOTCH PIES

Based on a recipe from Nancy Hubbard, these are just two creamy mouthfuls each.

Makes 2 dozen

⅓ **recipe Carlo's Cookie Dough (see page 33),** *or* **½ recipe Lemon–Cream Cheese Dough (page 50),** *or* **about 10 ounces of your favorite pie pastry dough**

BUTTERSCOTCH CREAM FILLING:

1½ **cups milk**
¼ **cup plus 2 tablespoons dark brown sugar**
2 **tablespoons cornstarch**
 Pinch of salt
2 **egg yolks**
1 **teaspoon pure vanilla extract**
1 **tablespoon cold unsalted butter**

TOPPING:

⅓ **cup heavy cream, whipped with 2 teaspoons confectioners' sugar and ¼ teaspoon pure vanilla extract until not quite stiff**

1. Roll the pastry dough on a lightly floured surface to a thickness of ¹⁄₁₆ inch. With a 3-inch fluted round cutter, cut out rounds of dough and fit them into ungreased miniature (1¾-inch) muffin tins. Reroll scraps of dough as necessary. Chill the pastry until firm, at least 30 minutes.

2. **BUTTERSCOTCH CREAM FILLING:** Heat 1¼ cups of the milk in a heavy saucepan until nearly boiling. Meanwhile, in a mixing bowl, whisk together the brown sugar, cornstarch, and salt until blended. Add the remaining ¼ cup cold milk and the egg yolks, whisking until smooth. Gradually mix the heated milk into the egg yolk mixture. Return the mixture to the saucepan and bring it to a boil, whisking constantly. Boil 1 minute, stirring; then strain into a mixing bowl. Stir in the vanilla and butter. Lay a sheet of plastic wrap or wax paper on the surface of the filling; set aside on a wire rack to cool.

3. **BAKING THE COOKIE SHELLS:** Preheat the oven to 350°F. Prick the pastry gently with a fork. Bake until the pastry is lightly golden and baked through, pricking any air bubbles with a fork, 12 to 15 minutes. Cool the cookie shells completely, in their tins, on a wire rack.

4. **ASSEMBLY:** With a table knife, carefully remove the shells from the tins. Whisk the cooled filling once or twice to smooth it out. Spoon about a tablespoon of the filling into each shell. Top each with a dab of whipped cream and chill briefly before serving. (*Note:* As these pies are best when eaten fairly soon after filling, fill only as many as you'll be serving at one time.)

CARAMELIZED ALMOND SPIRALS

Like miniature Danish pastries, very crisp and flaky. Like all pastries made with this dough, these should be eaten on the day they are baked. The assembled, sliced unbaked pastries can be wrapped and frozen, then baked directly from the freezer.

Makes 6 to 6½ dozen

½ recipe Incredibly Quick Puff Pastry Dough (see page 96), or a 17-ounce package frozen puff pastry dough, defrosted but still well chilled
1 cup sugar, plus more as needed
1 egg, lightly beaten
1 cup chopped almonds

1. Divide the dough in four equal pieces, cutting straight down with a large sharp knife. Keep three of the pieces of dough refrigerated while you roll the first piece.

2. Sprinkle 2 tablespoons of the sugar on a work surface. Roll out the dough on the sugar to a neat 10 × 6-inch rectangle about ⅜ inch thick. As you roll, turn the dough over once or twice to coat both sides with sugar. Lightly brush the surface of the rectangle with beaten egg; then sprinkle with 2 tablespoons of the sugar and ¼ cup of the chopped almonds. Roll a rolling pin gently over the surface of the dough, so that the sugar and almonds adhere. Starting with one of the short ends, roll up the dough tight, pressing the seam to seal. Wrap in plastic wrap, chill, and repeat with remaining dough. Chill about ½ hour to firm up the dough.

3. Preheat the oven to 375°F. Place a layer of sugar on a large plate or sheet of wax paper. Slice the rolls about ⅜ inch thick and dip both cut sides in the sugar, coating them very lightly. Place the slices, cut side down, on two ungreased baking sheets (nonstick sheets work well). Bake 9 or 10 minutes, or until the bottoms of the cookies are nicely glazed with caramel. Working quickly, turn the cookies over with a spatula. Continue to bake until both sides are nicely glazed, 5 or 6 minutes longer. (Watch these cookies carefully; they can burn easily.) Transfer to a wire rack to cool. Serve at room temperature or slightly warm.

INCREDIBLY QUICK PUFF PASTRY

Traditionally, puff pastry—the buttery, flaky dough used for Napoleons—is one of the most demanding pastries to make. A series of "turns"—rolling and folding the dough—produces alternating layers of dough and butter, which results in the flakiness that gives Napoleons their French name: *millefeuille* ("a thousand leaves").

This easy version is made in minutes, and produces excellent results. It freezes well, and can be used for all sorts of cookies, pastries, and hors d'oeuvre. Note that all puff pastry tastes best on the day it is baked. And to keep it crisp, don't refrigerate baked pastry.

Makes about 2¼ pounds

3 **cups flour**
¾ **teaspoon salt**
1 **pound plus 1 ounce (4 sticks plus 2 tablespoons) chilled unsalted butter, cut in ½-inch cubes**
¾ **cup cold water, or as needed**

1. Sift the flour and salt into a large mixing bowl. Cut in the butter, using two butter knives, a pastry blender, or your fingers. Leave the butter in large (about ¼-inch) chunks. Stir in just enough cold water to hold the dough together. At this point, the dough will look lumpy and not blended.

2. Transfer the dough to a floured work surface and roll out to a rectangle about 12 × 16 inches, with a short end facing you. Use a pastry scraper to fold the dough in thirds (as you would a letter). Now rotate the dough 90 degrees, so the open side is at your right. This entire procedure is called a single turn. Give the dough three more single turns, rolling it out each time to a 12 × 16-inch rectangle, folding in thirds, and rotating 90 degrees. Wrap the dough in plastic wrap and chill at least 2 hours or overnight. The puff pastry dough is now ready to use.

Note on Storing Puff Pastry Dough: The puff pastry dough will keep for about 3 days in the refrigerator, tightly wrapped, or can be frozen for up to 6 months. For convenience, cut pastry dough to be frozen in half or thirds, cutting straight down with a large chef's knife (to preserve the layering), then wrap each portion in plastic wrap. Place the portions in a plastic bag, label and date, and freeze. Defrost in the refrigerator until the dough is just malleable enough to be rolled out.

Other Miniatures:

Impossibly Rich Chocolate Pudding Cups, page 69
Cream Cheese & Jelly Turnovers, page 81
Lee Ann's Lemon-Orange Bars, page 118
Chocolate-Glazed Lebkuchen, page 128

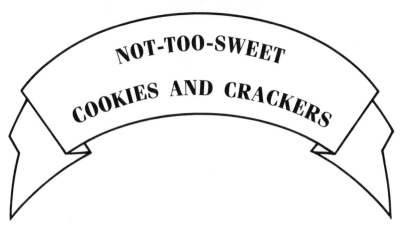

NOT-TOO-SWEET
COOKIES AND CRACKERS

Cinnamon-Honey Graham Crackers

Grandma's Mohn Moons

Toasted Sesame Biscuits

Nippy Three-Cheese Wafers

Whole-Grain Wafers

Other Not-Too-Sweet Cookies

Many of us grew up being given sweets as a "treat." Only later did we wean ourselves away from overly sweet edibles, which are not only not healthy for us, but don't taste very good. (Second-rate commercial bakeries hide the taste of inferior shortening with an excess of sugar.)

But that doesn't mean giving up the pleasures of cookies. In this chapter are cookies that are less sweet, along with several home-baked crackers. That's not to say, of course, that the rest of the cookies in this book are loaded with sugar. In all the recipes in this book, sugar quantities have been kept reasonable, to allow all the other good flavors to come through—spices, fruits, chocolate, vanilla, and especially, the sweet taste of fresh butter.

There are times, though, when you want a cookie that's more like a cracker— maybe the English word "biscuit" describes it best. These not-too-sweet cookies and crackers are good with tea or coffee, or served with cheese, or as a late-night snack, and may in fact be best for breakfast.

CINNAMON-HONEY GRAHAM CRACKERS

These are fun to press onto the baking pan—and taste fresher than any Graham cracker you can buy. You can also try dipping the baked, cooled Grahams in melted semisweet chocolate, coating them halfway (for instructions, see Black & White Butter Pretzels, p. 52).

Makes 2 dozen

3 tablespoons unsalted butter, softened
2 tablespoons solid vegetable shortening, softened
⅓ cup (packed) light brown sugar
2 tablespoons honey
2 teaspoons molasses
1⅓ cups whole wheat flour
4 teaspoons cornmeal
½ teaspoon cinnamon
½ teaspoon baking powder
⅛ teaspoon baking soda
½ teaspoon (scant) salt
4 teaspoons cold water, or as needed

TOPPING:

3 tablespoons sugar
¼ teaspoon cinnamon

1. In an electric mixer at medium-low speed, combine the butter, vegetable shortening, brown sugar, honey, molasses, whole wheat flour, cornmeal, cinnamon, baking powder, baking soda, salt, and water. Mix just until the dough begins to hold together (it will still look crumbly). Turn the machine off and press a piece of dough together between your fingers. If it crumbles apart, gradually add a little more cold water, until the dough just holds together when pressed, but isn't too moist.

2. With your fingers, press the dough onto a large, buttered baking sheet (without sides), patching as necessary to get an even, flat rectangle about 10 × 15 inches. (If you don't have a baking sheet without sides, you can use the underside of a jelly roll pan.) The dough will be very thin—barely ⅛ inch thick. Cover the dough with a sheet of wax paper and roll the dough smooth with a rolling pin. Chill until firm, at least 30 minutes.

3. Preheat the oven to 350°F. Carefully peel off the wax paper. Combine the sugar and cinnamon for the topping; sprinkle an even layer of the cinnamon

sugar over the surface of the dough. With a sharp knife or a dough scraper, trim off the edges of the dough. Using a ruler as a guide, cut the dough in 2½-inch squares, pushing the squares apart slightly with the knife. (As an easy guide, cut the sheet of dough in four long strips, and then divide each into six squares.) Prick each square three times with a fork.

4. Bake the crackers until lightly golden at the edges, about 12 minutes (watch carefully; these thin crackers can burn easily). Cool the Graham crackers on the baking sheet for about 2 minutes to firm them up, then transfer them carefully with a large spatula to a wire rack to cool completely (the crackers will become crisper as they cool). Store airtight, packing them gently to prevent breakage.

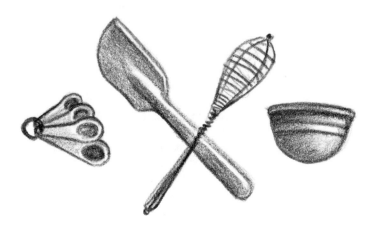

GRANDMA'S MOHN MOONS

When we visited my grandmother's kitchen as kids, we knew there would be some special treat around—her chocolate-and-walnut-covered banana cake, or these cookies, studded with poppy seeds. This recipe is based on one she hand-copied in the 1920s for *kichlach* (egg cookies). Because they're *pareve* (made without dairy products), these cookies can be served after a meat meal by people who observe the Jewish dietary laws.

Makes about 7 dozen

3 cups flour
1 tablespoon baking powder
Pinch of salt
1 cup (scant) sugar
½ cup vegetable oil
4 eggs
½ cup poppy seeds (2¼ ounces)

1. Sift the flour with the baking powder and salt into the bowl of an electric mixer (or any large mixing bowl). Make a well in the center of the flour, and fit the bowl into the mixer if you are using it.

2. Place the sugar, oil, eggs, and poppy seeds in the well. Mix until the dough is well blended. At this point, the dough may look slightly gray—that's OK. Place the dough on a floured sheet of plastic wrap, sprinkle with a little flour, and wrap. Chill until quite firm, at least 2 hours or overnight.

3. Preheat the oven to 350°F. Lightly butter three baking sheets (or sheets of aluminum foil); set aside. Divide the dough in four portions. Place one portion on a lightly floured work surface, leaving the remainder refrigerated. Roll out the dough to a thickness of ⅜ inch. Cut out 2- to 2½-inch crescents with a floured cookie cutter (you can find crescent-shape cutters, or cut crescents with a round biscuit cutter or a glass—which is what my grandmother used). Transfer the cookies to the baking sheets, spacing them not too far apart. Repeat with remaining dough.

4. Bake the cookies until the edges and bottoms are lightly golden, about 17 minutes. Transfer to a wire rack to cool. They keep well, stored airtight.

TOASTED SESAME BISCUITS

These are a hybrid—a combination of old South Carolina recipes for benne (sesame seed) cookies, and Italian sesame-coated biscuits. A crisp but tender biscuit, baked to a pale gold, with the haunting, toasty flavor of Oriental sesame oil. Try them with espresso or tea. These biscuits improve in flavor as they keep.

Makes 5 dozen 3-inch cookies

2½ **cups sesame seeds (about 12 ounces)**
2 **cups flour**
2 **teaspoons baking powder**
⅛ **teaspoon salt**
⅔ **cup light brown sugar**
½ **cup granulated sugar**
½ **cup (1 stick) unsalted butter, melted and cooled slightly**
2 **eggs**
2 **egg yolks**
2 **teaspoons Oriental sesame oil (optional) (available in Oriental and specialty groceries; do not substitute clear sesame oil)**
½ **teaspoon pure vanilla extract**

1. Preheat the oven to 300°F. Place the sesame seeds on a jelly roll pan and toast until lightly golden, stirring once or twice to toast evenly, about 10 minutes. (Watch carefully to prevent burning.) Set aside to cool; increase the oven heat to 350°F. Butter three baking sheets (or sheets of aluminum foil); set aside.

2. Place the remaining ingredients in an electric mixer bowl: the flour, baking powder, salt, brown and white sugars, butter, eggs, egg yolks, sesame oil, and vanilla. Add 1½ cups of the toasted sesame seeds and mix at medium-low speed just until the dough comes together. Let the dough stand at cool room temperature for about 10 minutes to firm up slightly.

3. Place the remaining sesame seeds in a cake or pie pan. Measure a level tablespoon of the dough, drop it into the pan of sesame seeds, and gently turn the dough over to coat with seeds while you shape it into a 2-inch oval "log" with tapered ends. Gently place the cookie on the baking sheet; repeat with remaining dough, spacing the cookies about 1 inch apart.

4. Bake until lightly golden, 11 to 13 minutes. Transfer to a wire rack to cool completely. These cookies improve on standing, and can be stored and mailed very well.

NIPPY THREE-CHEESE WAFERS

More a cracker than a cookie; just the thing with a glass of wine or beer. Careful—these are addictive. You can make this dough in quantity and keep the rolls of dough frozen. Whenever you'd like to put out "a little something" to nibble on, just defrost, slice, and bake as many as you need.

Makes about 6 dozen

10 tablespoons (1 stick plus 2 tablespoons) unsalted butter, softened
 6 ounces sharp Cheddar cheese, grated (about 3 cups, very loosely packed)
 3 ounces Swiss cheese, grated (about 1 cup)
½ cup (scant) fresh-grated Parmesan cheese
 1 tablespoon Dijon mustard
 3 tablespoons beer
2¼ cups flour
¾ teaspoon baking powder
¼ teaspoon baking soda
¼ teaspoon cayenne pepper
 1 cup fine-chopped walnuts

1. In an electric mixer at medium speed, cream the butter with the Cheddar, Swiss, and Parmesan cheeses until well blended. Mix in the mustard, then the beer.

2. Meanwhile, sift the flour, baking powder, baking soda, and cayenne onto a sheet of wax paper. Stir the walnuts into the flour mixture. Lower the mixer speed; add the dry ingredients, mixing just until blended, no longer.

3. Divide the dough in three portions; wrap each portion in plastic wrap, forming into a cylindrical shape. Twist the ends shut, pressing the dough toward the center of the roll to eliminate air pockets. Smooth the dough into neat rolls about 1½ inches thick and 9 inches long. Chill the rolls overnight, or at least 4 hours.

4. Preheat the oven to 350°F. Slice the rolls of dough ⅜ inch thick and transfer the rounds of dough to three ungreased baking sheets (or sheets of aluminum foil). Bake until the wafers are pale golden at the edges, about 15 minutes. Transfer to a wire rack and serve slightly warm or at room temperature. Store airtight for up to 4 days.

WHOLE-GRAIN WAFERS

These English digestive biscuits (don't be put off by the name) are similar to our Graham crackers, with a nutty flavor and crumbly texture all their own. They do good things for cheese, or you can make them into Whole-Grain Lemon Cream Sandwiches (see page 83).

Makes about 2 dozen

1½ **cups whole wheat flour**
⅓ **cup regular or quick-cooking oats (not instant oatmeal)**
3 **tablespoons light brown sugar**
1 **teaspoon baking powder**
½ **teaspoon salt**
6 **tablespoons (¾ stick) cold unsalted butter, cut in pieces**
3 **tablespoons milk, or more as needed**

1. Preheat the oven to 375°F. Lightly butter a baking sheet; set aside.

2. In a food processor or a mixing bowl, mix together the flour, oatmeal, brown sugar, baking powder, and salt. Cut in the butter, pulsing the processor on and off, until the mixture is crumbly. Add enough milk to make a cohesive but not sticky dough.

3. Roll out the dough on a lightly floured surface to a thickness of about ⅛ inch. Cut out 2¼-inch rounds with a plain or fluted round biscuit cutter. Place the rounds on the baking sheet; reroll scraps of dough and cut out remaining biscuits.

4. Bake until very lightly browned, 12 to 14 minutes. Transfer to a wire rack to cool. Store when completely cooled.

Other Not-Too-Sweet Cookies:

Anisette Toasts, page 126
Portuguese Almond Macaroons, page 130

GREAT MOMENTS IN COOKIE HISTORY: PART TWO

1930s   Ruth Wakefield introduces chocolate chip cookies at her Toll House Inn in Whitman, Massachusetts. Mrs. Wakefield cut a chocolate bar into bits and added them to the cookie dough, expecting them to melt. Instead, the chocolate held its shape, softening just slightly, and Toll House cookies were born. Mrs. Wakefield's original recipe appears on the back of every bag of Nestle's semisweet chocolate morsels, as it has since the 1940s. And it's still the best.

1939   Nestlé's chocolate morsels are introduced, changing American cookies forever. Today, more than 90 million bags are sold every year—which go into 150 million pounds of cookies, baked with Nestlé's morsels alone.

1956   Margaret Rudkin introduces her Pepperidge Farm line of "Distinctive Cookies." Mrs. Rudkin used Belgian recipes, after having tasted cookies all over Europe. Her insistence on high-quality ingredients (rare in commercially baked cookies) was a breakthrough for American cookie lovers.

Early 1970's   Andy Warhol is photographed with his cookie jar collection for *New York* Magazine. Cookie jars become popular again, as do other folk crafts.

1975   Famous Amos opens his walk-up cookie house on Sunset Boulevard, Hollywood—for people who can't wait for their "cookie hit."

1977   Mrs. Fields opens her first cookie store in Palo Alto, California. (As of late 1986, Debbie Fields's empire extends to well over 350 stores.)

June 1979   David Liederman (a lawyer who trained as a chef at a famed 3-star restaurant in France) opens the first David's Cookies store in New York City, and launches a cookie revolution:

1. Liederman brings back cookies with chocolate chunks rather than chips. While this was the start of a trend ("wonderfully copied all over the world," according to David), it actually harks back to the Ruth Wakefield days before morsels were invented, when people would cut up a chocolate bar to make chocolate chip cookies.

2. Liederman uses only top-quality Swiss chocolate, a daring choice at that time.

3. Liederman borrows a trick from Fauchon, the fancy food emporium in Paris: a special fan that blows the cookie fragrance out onto the sidewalk, enticing passersby by making them salivate.

1984   David's Cookies hits Tokyo.

1985   Sales of several commercial brands of "soft" cookies are a major disappointment to their manufacturers. Cookie lovers aren't surprised—soft, home-style cookies must be baked at home, and commercial versions, loaded with preservatives and inferior shortening, are no substitute.

Spring 1985   Mrs. Fields introduces white chocolate–macadamia nut cookies, creating an instant all-American classic.

1986   David's Cookies arrives in Paris, thus demonstrating to the world that real American cooking is as good as any in the world.

FOR COOKIE LOVERS WITH ARISTOCRATIC TASTES

Rich Walnut Sandies
Light-as-a-Breeze Linzer Wafers
Giant Orange-Almond Tiles
Lee Ann's Lemon-Orange Bars
Chocolate-Dipped Hazelnut Shortbread Wedges
Espresso Bars
More Aristocratic Cookies

Have you ever eaten at one of the great three-star restaurants of France, or the *luxe-luxe* ones in this country, such as The Four Seasons in New York? After your meal, after your dessert (selected from a decision-defying cart, or a soufflé cooked to order, or whatever indulgence suits your mood), there's a little surprise waiting for you, a little extra treat that I wish more restaurants would offer.

When your coffee is served, it is accompanied by a little silver tray covered with a doily. On it are several kinds of cookies—not *just* cookies, but extraordinary little mouthfuls: rich nut wafers; crackly meringues; crisp wafers curved to resemble French roof tiles; tiny, pop-in-your-mouth macaroons; and my favorites, miniature cookies made with crisp, buttery puff pastry. They're there as a little surprise "extra," like chocolate truffles.

Sitting there, sipping coffee in the glow that warms inside after a great meal, nibbling those "aristocratic" cookies is, for me, the best part of the whole experience.

RICH WALNUT SANDIES

Buttery-rich, loaded with nuts, and easy to make. A perfect after-dinner cookie.

Makes about 3 dozen

1 ¼ **cups walnuts (about 4 ounces)**
1 ½ **cups flour**
 ⅓ **cup granulated sugar**
 ⅓ **cup light brown sugar**
 ¾ **cup (1 ½ sticks) unsalted butter, softened slightly**
 ½ **teaspoon pure vanilla extract**
 ¾ **cup coarse-chopped walnuts (about 2 ounces)**

1. Place the 1 ¼ cups walnuts in a food processor with the flour and granulated sugar and process, pulsing the machine on and off, until the nuts are finely chopped. Add the brown sugar, butter, and vanilla; pulse the machine just until the dough comes together. It will be quite soft.

2. Divide the dough in half; wrap each portion in plastic wrap and form into a cylindrical shape. Twist the ends shut, pressing the dough toward the center of the roll to eliminate air pockets. Smooth the dough into neat rolls about 1 ½ inches thick. Chill the rolls for about 1 hour. Gently unwrap the rolls and coat the surfaces with the chopped walnuts, pressing them in gently. Re-wrap and chill until very firm, at least 2 hours.

3. Preheat the oven to 300°F. Lightly butter two baking sheets. Cut the dough in ¼-inch-thick slices. Place the cookies on the baking sheets, spacing them about 1 inch apart. Bake until golden, 10 to 12 minutes. Cool the cookies for a few minutes on the baking sheets; then very carefully transfer them to a wire rack and cool completely. (These cookies are fragile.) Store airtight.

LIGHT-AS-A-BREEZE LINZER WAFERS

Rich, rich, rich! A thin, crisp wafer version of the Austrian nut-based torte. These are tasty on their own, or with afternoon tea or after-dinner coffee.

Makes about 4½ dozen

11 **tablespoons (1 stick plus 3 tablespoons) unsalted butter, softened**
 2 **cups sifted confectioners' sugar**
    Grated zest of 1 small lemon
 1 **egg**
 1 **egg white**
 1 **cup ground hazelnuts, almonds, or a combination (about 4 ounces)**
1⅓ **cups flour**

1. Cream the butter with the confectioners' sugar and lemon zest in an electric mixer until very light, 3 to 5 minutes. Add the egg, then the egg white, mixing until smooth. Lower the mixer speed and add the ground nuts and the flour, mixing just until blended, no longer.

2. Divide the dough in half; wrap each portion in plastic wrap in a thick, cylindrical shape. Twist the ends shut, pressing the dough toward the center of the roll to eliminate air pockets. Smooth each portion of dough into a neat roll about 2 inches thick. Chill overnight, or at least 4 hours. (This dough is very rich, and can be handled only when well chilled.)

3. Preheat the oven to 350°F. Lightly butter two baking sheets. Cut the rolls of dough in ¼-inch-thick slices; then place the slices on the baking sheets, spacing them about 2 inches apart.

4. Bake the wafers until the edges are lightly golden, 10 to 12 minutes. Transfer the cookies immediately to a wire rack to cool. Store airtight.

GIANT ORANGE-ALMOND TILES

Because they are made with egg yolk rather than whites, these cookies are tenderer and more substantial than traditional French *tuiles,* which got their name from the roof tiles they resemble. This dough is slightly fragile and hard to handle, but it turns into the crispest, most buttery cookies you can imagine. These are a nice "extra" with strong coffee after a special dinner.

Makes 12 to 15

1   **cup flour**
½   **cup sugar**
½   **cup (1 stick) unsalted butter, softened**
1   **egg yolk**
2   **teaspoons grated orange zest (from 1 small orange)**
1   **tablespoon orange juice, preferably squeezed fresh**
½   **cup sliced almonds, or as needed (or substitute slivered or coarse-chopped almonds)**

1. Place the flour, sugar, butter, egg yolk, orange zest, and orange juice in an electric mixer at medium-low speed; mix just until the dough comes together. Wrap in plastic wrap and chill until firm, at least 2 hours.

2. Preheat the oven to 350°F. Divide the dough in three pieces. On a lightly floured board, roll out one piece of dough (leaving the remainder refrigerated) to a thickness of ⅛ inch. With a floured cookie cutter or a glass, cut out 4-inch rounds. With a floured spatula, transfer the rounds carefully to an ungreased baking sheet (or a sheet of foil), spacing them well apart—only four cookies will fit on each sheet. Sprinkle the cookies with almonds. Repeat with remaining dough while you bake the cookies, chilling and rerolling the scraps, too.

3. Bake the cookies until lightly browned at the edges, about 6 minutes. Once the cookies are out of the oven, you must work quickly, in order to shape them while they are still warm. First, let the cookies cool on the baking sheet for a minute or two, so they can be handled without falling apart. Then, very gently lift each cookie from the baking sheet and drape it over a rolling pin, forming a curved shape. (If you have narrow French

bread pans, you can also place them down the length of the curved pans.) Once the cookies have cooled, transfer them to a plate, so you can curve the remaining cookies. These cookies are very fragile; handle with care. (*Note:* If, once you take the cookies from the oven, they become too cool to curve easily, return them to the oven just until warm and supple, 1 minute or less; then shape as directed.)

LEE ANN'S LEMON-ORANGE BARS

Adapted from a recipe of my friend Lee Ann Fisher in New Jersey, a bar cookie—almost a miniature French tart—with the refreshing combination of lemon and orange. The chopped almonds make a crumbly crust, the sliced almonds give the top a neat, finished look.

Makes 3 dozen 2¼ × 1-inch bars

ALMOND CRUST:

- **1 cup less 2 tablespoons flour**
- **2 tablespoons chopped almonds**
- **½ cup (1 stick) unsalted butter, softened**
- **¼ cup confectioners' sugar**
- **⅛ teaspoon salt**
  Grated zest of ½ lemon (reserve the other half for the filling)

LEMON-ORANGE FILLING:

- **2 eggs**
- **¾ cup sugar**
  Grated zest of 1 orange
  Grated zest of ½ lemon
- **3 tablespoons orange juice, squeezed fresh**
- **2 tablespoons lemon juice, squeezed fresh**
- **2½ tablespoons flour**
- **½ teaspoon baking powder**
  Pinch of salt
- **¼ cup sliced almonds**

1. **ALMOND CRUST:** Preheat the oven to 375°F. Generously butter a 9-inch square baking pan. In a food processor or electric mixer, combine the flour, chopped almonds, butter, confectioners' sugar, salt, and lemon zest until they begin to form a cohesive dough. Pat the dough evenly into the bottom of the baking pan. Bake until lightly golden, 16 to 18 minutes.

2. **LEMON-ORANGE FILLING:** In a food processor, electric mixer, or mixing bowl, combine the eggs, sugar, orange and lemon zests, orange and lemon juices, flour, baking powder, and salt. Mix until pale and well combined.

3. When the crust is ready, remove the baking pan from the oven and lower the heat to 350°F. Pour the filling over the hot pastry; then sprinkle the sliced almonds on top. Bake until slightly puffed and lightly golden, about 20 minutes. Cool the pan on a wire rack; then use a sharp knife to cut the mixture into thirty-six 2¼ × 1-inch bars. (Make 8 cuts in one direction, 3 in the other.) Serve at cool room temperature.

CHOCOLATE-DIPPED HAZELNUT SHORTBREAD WEDGES

Easy to make, and excellent for gifts, as they mail well.

Makes 2 dozen wedges (two 8-inch rounds)

1¼ cups whole hazelnuts, with skins (about 5 ounces; other nuts can be substituted)
1¼ cups flour
½ cup plus 2 tablespoons sugar
Pinch of salt
10 tablespoons (1 stick plus 2 tablespoons) unsalted butter, melted and cooled slightly

CHOCOLATE GLAZE:

4 ounces semisweet chocolate, coarsely chopped (or substitute ⅔ cup semisweet chocolate morsels)
1 tablespoon solid vegetable shortening

1. Preheat the oven to 350°F. Butter and flour two 8-inch round cake or tart pans; set the pans aside.
2. Place the hazelnuts, flour, sugar, and salt in a food processor and pulse the machine on and off until the mixture is powdery. Pour in the butter and continue to pulse the machine until the mixture is well blended.
3. Divide the mixture evenly between the prepared pans, pressing it smooth. With a sharp knife, cut each round of dough into 12 wedges. Bake until the mixture is set and very pale tan, 20 to 23 minutes (do not overbake). Place the pans on a wire rack. While the shortbread is still warm, cut through the wedges again; cool slightly.
4. Choose a plate or paper plate slightly smaller than the cake pans; place the plate directly on the surface of each round of shortbread. Carefully invert the shortbread onto the plate.
5. CHOCOLATE GLAZE: Melt the chocolate and the vegetable shortening in the top of a double boiler, stirring occasionally, until smooth and glossy. Remove from heat; transfer to a paper cup or deep, narrow measuring cup (deep enough to dip the wedges in.)
6. Dip the tip of each wedge into the warm chocolate, coating it about halfway, and letting excess chocolate drip back into the cup. Place the dipped shortbread, right-side-up, on a wire rack over a sheet of wax paper. Cool until set.

ESPRESSO BARS

A rich, coffee-flavored bar cookie, glossed with chocolate: "brownies for adults."

Makes 32 bars, 1 × 2 inches

1 egg
⅔ cup light brown sugar
1 cup plus 2 tablespoons flour
¼ teaspoon baking powder
½ teaspoon baking soda
   Pinch of salt
2 tablespoons instant coffee
   powder, preferably instant
   espresso, Nescafé Brava, or
   other full-flavored coffee
2 teaspoons hot water
1½ teaspoons pure vanilla extract
½ cup (1 stick) unsalted butter,
   melted and cooled slightly
1 cup coarse-broken walnuts

ESPRESSO CHOCOLATE GLAZE:

4 ounces semisweet chocolate,
   coarsely chopped (or ⅔ cup
   semisweet chocolate morsels)
1 tablespoon strong brewed
   coffee, preferably hot
½ teaspoon instant coffee
   powder
1 tablespoon brandy or bourbon
1 teaspoon light corn syrup
2 tablespoons cold unsalted
   butter

1. Preheat the oven to 350°F. Butter and flour an 8-inch square baking pan; set aside.

2. In an electric mixer, whisk the egg and brown sugar at medium speed until light and fluffy, about 5 minutes. Meanwhile, sift the flour onto a sheet of wax paper with the baking powder, baking soda, and salt; set aside. In a small cup, stir together the instant coffee and hot water until smooth.

3. When the egg-sugar mixture is ready, lower the mixer speed and add the coffee mixture, vanilla, and melted butter, mixing just until blended. Add the flour mixture, mixing just until blended, no longer. Stir in the walnuts just until evenly distributed. Scrape the mixture into the baking pan, spreading it to the edges.

4. Bake 25 minutes, or just until a toothpick inserted in the center emerges clean. Cool on a wire rack.

5. ESPRESSO CHOCOLATE GLAZE: Melt the chocolate in the top of a double boiler over hot (not boiling) water, stirring occasionally until smooth. Remove from heat. In a small cup, stir the liquid coffee with the instant coffee powder until dissolved. Stir the coffee mixture, the brandy, corn syrup, and butter into the chocolate, until smooth and glossy. Spread the warm chocolate mixture over the surface of the espresso bars, coating evenly. Let stand at room temperature until the chocolate has set. Cut into neat 2 × 1-inch bars, using a knife dipped frequently in hot water.

More Aristocratic Cookies:

Maida Heatter's Oatmeal Wafers, page 38
Lemon–Cream Cheese Cookies (cut out with a shell-shaped cutter), page 50
Spumette, page 63
Impossibly Rich Chocolate Pudding Cups, page 69
The World's Best Rogelach, page 88
New York Cheesecake Squares, page 92
Virginia Hazelnut Bars, page 93
Caramelized Almond Spirals, page 95
Toasted Sesame Biscuits, page 105
Nippy Three-Cheese Wafers, page 106
Anisette Toasts, page 126
Chocolate-Glazed Lebkuchen, page 128
Portuguese Almond Macaroons, page 130
Hungarian Apricot-Walnut Slices (Gerbeaud Slices), page 131
Swedish Dream Cookies, page 134
Greek Almond Crescents (Kourambiedes), page 135

COOKIES FROM
AROUND THE WORLD

Anisette Toasts
Chocolate-Glazed Lebkuchen
Portuguese Almond Macaroons
Hungarian Apricot-Walnut Slices (Gerbeaud Slices)
Swedish Dream Cookies
Greek Almond Crescents (Kourambiedes)
More Cookies from Around the World

Traveling to other countries, some tourists head for art museums, some for cathedrals, some for famous sites from history. Not cookie lovers.

They poke their heads into bakeries, little grocery shops where even the canned goods are fascinating, and other new adventures in the perpetual pursuit of great cookies and other foods. And they often find an institution that we seldom see here, alas—the *patisserie-café, salon de thé,* or *Konditorei.* These shops are like our bakeries, except that on one side of the room, opposite the glass cases filled with temptations, there are neat little tables and chairs, so you can enjoy them on the spot.

Forget the éclairs and tartlets. Go up to the case and ask for a plate of assorted cookies—a couple hundred grams, say. Pick out exactly the ones you want, order coffee or hot chocolate, and sit down and enjoy yourself.

Here are a few cookie recipes I've gathered on "research trips."

ANISETTE TOASTS

A delicious version of a simple Italian cookie—crisp and dry, with a delicate sugar-spice coating and rich almond-anise flavor. Serve these for breakfast, or dip them into a late-afternoon cup of espresso or tea.

Makes 4 dozen

4 eggs
¾ cup sugar
Zest of 1 small lemon
1 cup coarse-chopped almonds
(about 4 ounces)
1½ cups flour
¼ teaspoon baking powder
Pinch of salt
4 teaspoons anise seeds,
crushed coarse
3 tablespoons Sambuca or
anisette liqueur

TOPPING:

1 egg white, lightly beaten
2 tablespoons sugar
¼ teaspoon cinnamon

1. Preheat the oven to 350°F. Lightly grease two baking sheets; set aside.

2. In an electric mixer (with the whisk attachment), beat the eggs, sugar, and lemon zest at medium speed until the mixture forms a thick ribbon when dropped from the whisk, about 5 minutes.

3. Meanwhile, pulse the almonds in a food processor with the flour, baking powder, salt, and anise seeds until the almonds are finely chopped. (Do not overprocess, or the nuts will be ground. These cookies should have a slight crunch.)

4. When the egg mixture is ready, remove the mixing bowl from the mixer and gently fold in the Sambuca or anisette. Now fold in the almond mixture, adding it in four portions. Spoon the mixture into logs about 2 inches wide and as long as the baking sheets, placing two logs on each sheet, and spacing them well apart.

5. Bake until lightly golden, about 20 minutes. Remove the baking sheets from the oven.

6. TOPPING: Gently brush the logs with a light coating of egg white. Stir together the sugar and cinnamon; sprinkle this over the logs. Now slice the logs diagonally 1 inch thick (if your baking sheets are non-stick, carefully transfer the baked logs with two spatulas to a cutting surface, slice them, and return the slices to the baking sheets).

7. Return the slices to the oven, topping upward, and bake until crisp and golden, about 8 minutes longer. Transfer the biscuits to a wire rack and cool. These cookies keep well, stored airtight. They can also be mailed, packed with crumpled wax paper to prevent breakage.

CHOCOLATE-GLAZED LEBKUCHEN

A stellar German cookie, freely adapted from a recipe of Doris Langsdorf. These are small, chewy chocolate-glazed diamonds or squares, moist with honey, and with deep, spicy flavor. They'll make you think of being home for the winter holidays, sitting around the fireplace, and all sorts of other good things. (Note that this dough must be made a day in advance, to let the flavors mellow and ripen.)

Makes 2 to 3 dozen pieces

¾ cup sugar
½ cup plus 1 tablespoon honey
1 tablespoon water
4 tablespoons (½ stick)
   unsalted butter, cut in pieces
¾ cup chopped almonds (with
   skins)
⅓ cup fine-chopped candied or
   dried pineapple (or any other
   good candied fruit)
⅓ cup lightly beaten egg (a little
   more than 1 large egg)
3 tablespoons orange juice
½ teaspoon almond extract
1⅔ cups sifted flour
1 teaspoon baking powder
½ teaspoon baking soda
1½ teaspoons cinnamon
1½ teaspoons ground cardamom
½ teaspoon (generous) ground
   cloves
½ teaspoon freshly grated
   nutmeg
½ teaspoon ground ginger

1. Make the dough 1 day before you plan to bake the lebkuchen. Combine the sugar, honey, water, and butter in a large heavy saucepan. Bring just to a boil, stirring to dissolve the sugar. The moment the mixture begins to boil, remove the pan from heat and add the almonds, candied fruit, beaten egg, orange juice, and almond extract, stirring until the mixture is smooth.

2. Place a sifter over a sheet of wax paper; re-sift the flour with the baking powder, baking soda, cinnamon, cardamom, cloves, nutmeg, and ginger. Add this mixture to the saucepan, stirring just until the ingredients are well blended. Place a sheet of wax paper on the surface of the dough and cool thoroughly. Seal with plastic wrap or aluminum foil and let stand at room temperature overnight. Do *not* refrigerate.

3. Preheat the oven to 350°F. Butter and flour a 9-inch square baking pan. With a large rubber spatula, place portions of the dough over the surface of the pan, then spread it as smooth as possible. (The dough will be quite sticky. If you like, you can pat the dough even with lightly floured fingertips, then brush off excess flour.) Bake until the surface has set, the sides have begun to shrink from the pan, and a toothpick inserted in the

CHOCOLATE GLAZE:

3 ounces semisweet chocolate, chopped (or substitute ½ cup semisweet chocolate morsels)

1½ teaspoons unsalted butter

1½ tablespoons boiling water

center of the lebkuchen emerges not quite clean, 27 to 29 minutes. Cool the pan on a wire rack.

4. **CHOCOLATE GLAZE:** Melt the chocolate over hot water. Add the butter, then the boiling water, stirring until completely smooth. Spread the glaze over the cooled surface of the lebkuchen. Let cool until the glaze has set.

5. Using a sharp knife and a ruler as a guide, cut the lebkuchen in neat diamonds or squares. (For diamonds, cut the pastry in six horizontal strips; then cut across at a sharp diagonal. For squares, cut the pan of cookies in six strips in each direction.) Lebkuchen keep well, getting better as they age, and can be mailed.

PORTUGUESE ALMOND MACAROONS

Based on a recipe for Portuguese macaroons called *bolos d'amendoas,* these little mouthfuls are chock-full of almonds. They're not as sweet as most macaroons, and the bread crumbs give them a nice crumbly texture. If possible, use homemade bread crumbs (made with crustless French or Italian bread, in the food processor or blender).

Makes about 4 dozen

1⅓ **cups whole almonds, with skins (6½ to 7 ounces)**
⅔ **cup dry bread crumbs, homemade if possible**
1 **cup plus 2 tablespoons sugar**
2 **tablespoons unsalted butter, melted**
½ **teaspoon almond extract**
4 **egg whites**
 Slivered or halved blanched almonds, for the tops

1. Preheat the oven to 325°F. Butter two baking sheets; set aside.

2. Place the whole almonds, bread crumbs, and sugar in a food processor and process until very finely chopped, but not ground to a smooth powder. (You can also do this in a blender, but you'll have to work in small batches.) Add the melted butter, almond extract, and egg whites, processing until well blended.

3. With dampened palms, roll the mixture into balls, using a rounded teaspoonful of dough for each cookie. Place the balls on the baking sheets in neat rows and gently press an almond sliver or half into each one, flattening it very slightly.

4. Bake the macaroons 17 minutes, until barely colored to a very pale gold. Transfer to a wire rack to cool; then store. These macaroons keep well for several days, stored airtight; they also mail well.

HUNGARIAN APRICOT-WALNUT SLICES

(Gerbeaud Slices)

In Hungary, the old tradition of the elegant coffee house, where people congregate over coffee to enjoy a piece of pastry and the latest gossip, is still very much alive, especially at the Café Vörösmarty in Budapest, which everyone has called Gerbeaud since Swiss-born Emile Gerbeaud took it over in 1884.

Although recently reconstructed, the elegant period interior of the café, with its cane chairs, marble-topped tables, and Maria Theresa chandeliers, has been faithfully preserved. And business carries on briskly. On a recent visit to Budapest, in fact, it was hard to find an empty table at Gerbeaud to enjoy one of the more than one hundred tortes, small pastries, yeast cakes, and ice creams prepared by some five to six dozen pastry cooks.

"Oh, there would be a public uproar if we shut down!" exclaimed Mária Ágoston-Reich, the engaging manager. "Many businessmen come here; it's a much more pleasant atmosphere for negotiations. And it's a traditional meeting place for dating couples. Ladies who have emigrated write to their Hungarian friends, and they all gather here to read the latest news from America. Then, they write back together as they sip their coffee—it's a regular Saturday and Sunday program!"

The recipe that follows is a simplified adaptation of the signature pastry served at Gerbeaud. In Budapest, it is made with a yeast dough; I've substituted a cream cheese pastry dough that's easier to work with. (See the Note following the recipe for a richer variation topped with a smooth chocolate glaze.)

Makes 27 bars, 1 × 3 inches

(continued)

RICH PASTRY DOUGH:

- ½ **cup (1 stick) unsalted butter, softened**
- 4 **ounces (½ cup) cream cheese, softened**
- ¾ **cup sugar**
- 1 **egg yolk**
- 1½ **teaspoons pure vanilla extract**
- ¼ **teaspoon salt**
- 2¼ **cups flour**

FILLING:

- ½ **cup dried apricots (about 2¼ ounces)**
- 1½ **cups walnuts (about 5½ ounces)**
- 1 **pound tart apples (e.g., 2 large Granny Smiths)**
- 1 **teaspoon fresh lemon juice**
- 1 **10-ounce jar apricot preserves**
- 4 **tablespoons (½ stick) unsalted butter, softened**
  Grated zest of ½ lemon

GLAZE:

Milk
Granulated sugar

1. **RICH PASTRY DOUGH:** Cream the butter, cream cheese, and sugar in an electric mixer at medium speed. Add the egg yolk, then the vanilla and salt, mixing until smooth. Lower the mixer speed and add the flour, mixing just until blended, no longer. Wrap the pastry dough in plastic wrap and chill until firm, at least 2 hours.

2. Divide the pastry in two slightly unequal portions; wrap and return the larger one to the refrigerator. Roll out the smaller portion on a lightly floured surface to a rough square shape about ⅛ inch thick. Using a 9-inch square baking pan as a guide, cut out a square of pastry and set aside the trimmings. Butter the baking pan; gently fit the square of pastry in the bottom; set aside. Roll the larger piece of pastry about ¼ inch thick; cut a 9-inch square and place it on a sheet of foil; chill both pieces of pastry while you make the filling. (The trimmings can be rerolled, baked until lightly golden, and eaten as cookies.)

2. **FILLING:** Place the dried apricots in a small bowl and cover with boiling water. Set aside until quite soft, about 15 minutes.

4. Preheat the oven to 375°F., with racks in the lower third and center levels of the oven.

5. In a food processor, pulse the walnuts until chopped coarse; transfer to a mixing bowl. Peel, quarter, and core the apples, then grate them. There should be about 2 cups. Sprinkle with lemon juice and stir into the walnuts. Set aside 2 tablespoons strained apricot preserves to glaze the finished pastry. Drain the soaked apricots and place them in the food processor with the remaining preserves. Process until smooth. Add the butter and lemon zest and process just until smooth, no longer. Add the apricot mixture to the mixing bowl and stir to combine the filling ingredients.

6. **ASSEMBLY**: Transfer the filling mixture to the pastry-lined baking pan, smoothing the surface with a spatula. Cut the other chilled square of pastry into ¾-inch-wide strips. Form a lattice by laying half the strips diagonally across the filling at even intervals; lay the remaining strips on top, placing them across at a sharp angle. Neatly trim excess pastry. Brush the pastry gently with milk; then sprinkle the entire surface with a light coating of sugar.

7. Bake on the lower oven rack for 20 minutes. Transfer the baking pan to the center oven rack and bake until the pastry is nicely golden, 10 to 15 minutes longer. Cool the pan on a wire rack. While still warm, gently brush the surface of the pastry and filling with the reserved strained preserves; cool completely. To serve, run a paring knife around the edges of the pan. With a sharp knife, trim off the edges, then cut the pastry in 3 neat strips in one direction, then at 1-inch intervals in the other. Serve at room temperature.

Note: If you'd like to make Gerbeaud's extra-rich variation, proceed as follows: Instead of forming a pastry lattice on top (in Step 6), top the filling with a solid sheet of the pastry. Bake until golden (as directed in Step 7), then cool in the pan. Run a small knife around the edges of the cooled pastry and carefully invert it onto a baking sheet. Brush the smooth top (formerly the bottom) with about 2 tablespoons apricot jam; let set.

Now melt 3 ounces chopped semisweet chocolate (or ½ cup semisweet chocolate morsels) over hot water with ½ teaspoon solid vegetable shortening. When the apricot glaze has set, brush the top with a smooth layer of chocolate; let set. With a long, serrated knife blade, neatly trim off edges of pastry, then cut in neat 3 × 1-inch bars.

SWEDISH DREAM COOKIES

Mmmm . . . the browned butter really does give these sandy cookies—in Swedish, they are called *drömmar*—a special flavor.

Makes about 5 dozen 1¼-inch cookies

1 cup (2 sticks) unsalted butter
¾ cup sugar
2 teaspoons pure vanilla extract
2 cups flour
1 teaspoon baking powder
30 to 35 blanched almonds, separated in halves

1. Butter two baking sheets; set aside. Melt the butter in a small heavy skillet, then cook until lightly browned, about 15 minutes (timing can vary). Watch carefully; don't let the butter get too dark. Transfer the browned butter to a small mixing bowl; stir in the sugar. Place the bowl in a larger bowl of ice water; stir the butter mixture until cooled and nearly firm.

2. Preheat the oven to 300°F. In an electric mixer or by hand, cream the butter mixture until light; add the vanilla. Meanwhile, sift the flour and baking powder together; add this mixture to the butter, mixing just until the ingredients are blended.

3. Roll rounded teaspoonfuls of the dough into uniform balls. Place on the baking sheets, spacing the balls 1 inch apart. Gently press an almond half into each ball. Bake the cookies until set and pale gold, about 20 minutes.

4. Transfer the cookies to a wire rack to cool completely; then store airtight.

GREEK ALMOND CRESCENTS

(Kourambiedes)

Slightly tricky to make, but the melt-in-your-mouth texture makes it worth it. Most classic Greek recipes call for blanched almonds; I prefer to use unblanched whole almonds (either is fine). With thanks to Barbara Livadas Fript.

Makes about 56 crescents

¾ cup whole unblanched almonds (about 3¾ ounces)
1 cup confectioners' sugar
2 3-inch strips orange zest, removed with a vegetable peeler
1 cup (2 sticks) unsalted butter, softened
1 egg yolk
¼ cup brandy
2 tablespoons orange juice, preferably squeezed fresh
⅜ teaspoon almond extract
1¾ cups all-purpose flour
½ cup cake flour
½ teaspoon baking powder

1. Grind the almonds with the confectioners' sugar and orange zest in a food processor until powdery. (You can also grind the nuts with a Mouli grater, then mix the dough in an electric mixer, or by hand.)

2. Add the butter, egg yolk, brandy, orange juice, almond extract, all-purpose flour, cake flour, and baking powder. Pulse the processor on and off just until the dough comes together, no longer.

3. Transfer the dough to a sheet of plastic wrap; dust lightly with flour. Chill until firm enough to handle, at least 1 hour.

4. Preheat the oven to 350°F. Lightly grease two baking sheets. Using a scant tablespoonful of dough for each cookie, form the dough into 3-inch-long ropes with tapered ends. Place the pieces on a baking sheet, curving the ropes around gently to form horseshoe shapes.

5. Bake the cookies until the edges are light brown, 14 or 15 minutes. Transfer to a wire rack placed over a sheet of wax paper. Dust the cookies generously with confectioners' sugar while they are still warm. Cool completely; then store. If necessary, sprinkle the cookies with a little more confectioners' sugar once they've cooled. Store airtight.

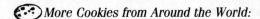 *More Cookies from Around the World:*

A FEW SPECIAL WAYS TO ENJOY COOKIES

- While they're still warm, rush a few cookies to a cookie-loving friend, so you can enjoy them together.
- Reward yourself with a few cookies after exercising.
- Take a bunch of cookies with you to the movies.
- Take a batch of home-baked cookies on a hike, to keep up your energy.
- Wrap a few cookies in a plastic bag and take them along on a car trip.
- Put a few cookies and milk beside your bed and curl up with a good book (cookies taste best when eaten while wearing pajamas).
- Bring along a plate of cookies the next time you're invited to a friend's house for dinner. Some people might bring a bottle of wine, but cookie lovers know what people *really* like to get.
- Have a cookie party with a group of friends—each one bakes his or her favorite cookies, and brings them for everyone to enjoy.
- Sneak down to the kitchen at midnight, and treat yourself to a few cookies with some milk or hot chocolate. Best way to relax before sleeping . . .
- Or pack up some cookies and go for a long walk, when you want to be all by yourself.

ACKNOWLEDGMENTS

I'd like to extend thanks to the following, all of whom generously provided support during the preparation of this book:

Barbara Campbell, Nestlé

Van Leer Family American Chocolate

Janet Turnbough, Pet Foods, for advice on cooking with granola

Trudye Connolly and Tom Traska, for information on Du Pont SilverStone Premium Non-Stick Surface

Joan Whitman

Sandy Gluck

Claire Reich

Susan Lescher

I've indicated in the text where recipes have been shared by good cooks. I thank them all for their generosity.

Rick Kot is a rare editor, unique in my experience. He invests as much energy in his books as his authors do—and I'm grateful (and frequently amazed) at my good fortune in being able to work with him.

Ruth Cousineau not only tested all the recipes in this book with me—some again and again—but also never failed to come up with good ideas, suggestions for improvement, and a lighthearted outlook that made working on this book together a pleasure. Thanks, Ruth.

INDEX

ABOUT THE AUTHOR

Richard Sax recently wrote *From the Farmers' Market* (with Sandra Gluck; Harper & Row), a cookbook with recipes and recollections from America's farm kitchens. He also stars in the video cookbook *Secrets for Great Dinner Parties* (Baffico/Breger Video).

Richard Sax contributes frequently to several national publications, including *Gourmet, Bon Appétit, Food & Wine, Elle, Working Woman, Ms., Good Food,* and *Yankee.*

A trained chef, Richard Sax spent two years in London as consultant to the Time-Life cookbook series *The Good Cook,* and was test kitchen chef for *Food & Wine* magazine during its initial two years. He makes frequent personal and television appearances throughout the U.S.

Richard Sax is also the author of *New York's Master Chefs,* the companion volume to the successful PBS television series; *Old-Fashioned Desserts;* and *Cooking Great Meals Every Day* (with David Ricketts). He lives in New York City and is a veteran cookie baker.